everything

TASTES BETTER WITH

GARLIC

everything
TASTES BETTER WITH
GARLIC
Positively Irresistible Recipes

by Sara Perry
photographs by France Ruffenach

CHRONICLE BOOKS
SAN FRANCISCO

LIBRARY OF CONGRESS CATALOGING-IN-
  PUBLICATION AVAILABLE.
ISBN: 0-8118-3816-1
MANUFACTURED IN HONG KONG
DESIGNED BY SARA SCHNEIDER
FOOD STYLING BY AMY NATHAN
PROP STYLING BY SARA SLAVIN

DISTRIBUTED IN CANADA BY
RAINCOAST BOOKS
9050 SHAUGHNESSY STREET
VANCOUVER, BRITISH COLUMBIA V6P 6E5

10 9 8 7 6 5 4 3 2 1

CHRONICLE BOOKS LLC
85 SECOND STREET
SAN FRANCISCO, CALIFORNIA 94105
WWW.CHRONICLEBOOKS.COM

DEDICATION

To my dear friends at Chronicle Books—Bill LeBlond, Amy Treadwell, Leslie Jonath, Michele Fuller, and Mikyla Bruder—you've made my life rich and savory and definitely sweet.

ACKNOWLEDGMENTS

Thanks go to the many chefs and cooks I have interviewed over the years for the *Oregonian*'s TasteMaker column and to those friends and colleagues who generously shared their ideas, expertise, time, and recipes, especially Jane Zwinger, Suzy Kitman, Karen Brooks, Kathlyn Meskel, Susan Friedland, chef Randall Cronwell, chef Eric Laslow, chef Leather Storrs, chef Jeanne Subotnick, Betty Rosbottom, and Sharon Maasdam. To copy editor Rebecca Pepper, who helped me mind my p's and q's. To Karen Kirtley, whose editorial eye, attention to detail, love of words, and warm friendship are invaluable. To France Ruffenach and her team for creating such beautiful photographs. And to Sara Schneider for her serene, elegant, and lively sense of style and design.

CONTENTS

GARLIC: LUSTY, LEGENDARY, AND POSITIVELY IRRESISTIBLE

Imagine cooking without it. Who would onions play with? What would happen to Italian food? Caesar salad? *Pistou?* Life without garlic? Impossible.

Think about it—everything tastes better with garlic. Well, almost everything. The world may have yet to invent a fabulous garlic-tiered tiramisù, but make no mistake: lines form deep and wide for garlic ice cream at the Gilroy Garlic Festival.

Garlic is the spice of life, the herb of choice, and the vegetable we all love to eat, rolled into one many-cloved bundle. It even comes gift-wrapped in papery tissue. What more could you ask for?

To love garlic, to completely give yourself over to its glory, is to banish all worries about breath and bad odors. Garlic tastes fabulous. I repeat: Garlic tastes fabulous. Its magic fills your mouth with a fantastic flavor. As for the smell, heck, it's downright perfume. The beauty of garlic is that it can be as sweet and delicate as a first kiss or as lively and lusty as an all-night orgy. It's all in the way it is wooed.

Cooks have always known that garlic adds distinctive flavor, earthy aroma, and subtle nuance to classic cuisines and everyday foods. It's pungent while raw, mellow when cooked, rich and nutty when roasted and caramelized—the more you fool around with garlic, the more it fools around with you. A single clove minced to a teaspoon adds a potent message to salad dressing, while a whole bulb left to simmer in a stew lends a subtle, meaningful undertone. With garlic, pastas pulsate; soups and sauces soar; meats, poultry, and seafood rise up and sing; and the vegetables all get eaten. More than any flavoring, garlic has the power to substitute for salt and the strength to stimulate the palate.

According to myth and legend, there is little garlic cannot do. Worn around the neck, the mystical bulb is mightier than the sword as a vampire slayer. Pressed to make a potion, it can banish disorders and infections. Hung in bunches on the door of a bride-to-be, it guarantees a blissful union. And when planted around roses, it makes aphids drop like flies. No wonder King Tut stashed six bulbs in his tomb for the afterlife.

Everything Tastes Better with Garlic is here to help you unravel the marvels of garlic. It explains the ways to peel, press, smash, slice, cut, and chop garlic, and it includes photographs to show you how each form should look. Why? Because garlic's effect on a dish depends on how you first prepare it. A table of garlic equivalents helps you know that when a dish calls for 2 tablespoons of chopped garlic, you'll need 4 large cloves, or when a recipe needs 1 minced medium clove, you'll end up with a firmly-packed 3/4 teaspoon.

Don't hold your breath, but *Everything Tastes Better with Garlic* aims to set the record straight on the odor question. What causes it? What do people do about it? You'll find answers to these and other nagging little questions: What's that little green thing sprouting from a clove, and what do I do with it? Can I use the garlic braid that's been hanging on my kitchen wall for more years than I can remember?

Everything Tastes Better with Garlic has more than 65 recipes. They're simple, they're delicious, and they're full of great garlic flavor. Treasured favorites like Caesar salad, garlic mashed potatoes, chicken with forty cloves, and old-fashioned garlic bread are here for the asking, along with sassy newcomers such as Spring Vegetable Soup with Toasted Garlic Bread Crumbs and Grilled T-Bone Steaks with Garlic Bourbon Barbecue Sauce. (There's even a yummy "Let's Feel Better" Broth, for when you need to play Dr. Mom.)

You'll search for any excuse to entertain so you can treat yourself to Beef Tenderloin with Port Garlic Sauce, Garlic Risotto with Baby Peas and Truffle Oil, or Pan-Roasted Seafood with Smoky Paprika and Roasted Garlic. (Sure, company will be just as happy with Six Cloves Mac and Cheese or Coney Island Hot Dogs with Damn-Good Garlic Sauce served with Crispy Garlic Potato Chips. Wouldn't you?)

I used to think all garlic was created equal and came dressed in white. But a world of fashionable garlic is out there waiting to be discovered—garlic of various colors, sizes, shapes, and tastes. To help you explore garlic in its many guises, I've included a handy resource guide with farms and garden sources, a year-round calendar of garlic festivals, tips on interesting books and savvy Web sites. So get ready for some fun and some great-tasting garlic.

Let's face it. In a world where you crave what tries to kill you, or at least to harden your arteries, garlic is one of those rare addictions that is actually good for you. Hmm—garlic martini anyone? With this versatile bulb, anything goes.

GOODNESS, GRACIOUS, GREAT BULBS OF GARLIC

"What's in a bulb anyway?" she asked with bated breath

WHAT IS GARLIC?

Garlic is a plant that makes the world a more flavorful place. It belongs to the lily family (that's right: it's a kissing cousin of those fragrant, showy lilies growing in your garden). With its characteristically compact, underground bulb, garlic shares the same genus *(Allium)* with onions, leeks, chives, and shallots. For our enjoyment, this herbaceous perennial is grown as an annual and harvested each year. If it were left in the ground—and not harvested for us to eat—the bulb would produce a stalk with white flowers and seeds, year after year. When divided, those familiar bulbs give us papery, perfumed packets of earthy delight, otherwise known as cloves.

Garlic has been cultivated for thousands of years, so it is not surprising that there are many varieties that differ in pungency, taste, size, shape, and color. *Allium sativum* is the garlic we use most often in cooking; within that grouping are the cultivated "softneck" *(sativum)* and "hardneck" *(ophioscorodon)* subgroups.

Next time you touch the top of a garlic head, feel for a hard stick in the middle. If it isn't there, you're holding a softneck.

Widely available in supermarkets, softneck varieties are easier to grow than hardneck varieties and offer the longest shelf life. Their skin is usually white or silvery. The two classic softneck varieties are called 'California Late' and 'California Early'. Others include 'Creole', 'Egyptian', and the milder 'Italian'.

Hardneck garlic (the kind that has the stick in the middle) is more perishable, so you're apt to spot more of these varieties at local farmers' markets or in a supermarket's specialty produce section in the summer and early fall. Their cloves are usually bigger (and easier to peel) than those of softneck garlic and have a wider color and flavor range. 'Spanish Roja', a red-skinned Oregon heirloom with an earthy taste, is the best-selling hardneck; others include 'Armenian', 'Mazatlán', and 'La Panant Kari', originally from the Republic of Georgia.

Elephant garlic *(Allium ampeloprasum)*, those enormous bulbs next to the normal-size ones, are more closely related to leeks than to garlic. Milder in taste, with a coarser texture, the 1-pound Goliaths have a following of their own.

WHAT'S IN A BULB, ANYWAY?

Garlic is rich in minerals, especially sulfur compounds. It also contains potassium, calcium, phosphorous, iron, riboflavin, and vitamin C. It has protein and carbohydrates. It is low in sodium and free of fat. An average clove has 2 calories. In other words, garlic is good food for the body.

GARLIC IS BREATHTAKING

Some say that eating too much garlic is like drinking too much champagne: it tastes great going down, but afterwards, you swear you'll *never* do that again. The reason for this angst? The culprit is sulfur.

While certain sulfur compounds are responsible for garlic's antibacterial activities, others cause strong, smelly garlic breath. This happens because once a raw clove is crushed, an enzyme sets off a chain reaction that creates the stinking sulfur compound. When it hits the digestive system and permeates the lungs and other tissues, it emits a familiar and unpleasant odor. Although thorough cooking destroys the enzyme, there is no foolproof way to completely eliminate the cause, so people continue to lick the backs of their hands, wait 30 seconds, and then smell them, or to ask the opinion of a friend or young child who'll tell it like it is. If "yes" is the answer to "Do I reek of garlic?" check out "Don't Hold Your Breath!" on the facing page to see if any of the traditional tonics are worth a try.

COULD SOMETHING SO GOOD BE GOOD FOR YOU?

Garlic flavors the food we love, and research suggests that it does a lot more when we eat it. Garlic is believed to lower cholesterol, control high blood pressure, and help prevent cancer. It also acts as a natural blood thinner, antifungal agent, and antibiotic. Formulas in the ancient Egyptian medical papyrus *Codex Eber* pointed to garlic's positive effects on heart problems, tumors, and childbirth. At Henry V's birth in 1387, his lips were anointed with garlic in the belief that its antiseptic powers would stimulate and protect the infant. And the twenty-first-century *Archives of Internal Medicine* reported on garlic's small but beneficial influence on cholesterol levels. So, whether or not you believe you can cure baldness by rubbing oil infused with garlic onto the affected area three times a day, you'll have to agree that garlic's curative powers over the centuries have been as engaging and promising as its culinary ones. (For more in-depth information about garlic's therapeutic benefits, see "Sources," page 126.)

DON'T HOLD YOUR BREATH!

Tips for the tainted

Chew a roasted coffee bean;
chew a raw fennel seed;
chew a fresh sprig of parsley.

Use toothpaste;
use mouthwash;
use a minty lozenge.

Drink some whiskey;
drink something stronger.
Then eat more garlic, with a close friend.

KINGDOM:	Plant
DIVISION:	Anthophyta
CLASS:	Monocotyledones
SUPERORDER:	Lilliiflorae
ORDER:	Asparagales
FAMILY:	Alliaceae
GENUS:	*Allium*
SPECIES:	*sativum*
SUBSPECIES:	*sativum* ("softneck" varieties)
	ophioscorodon ("hardneck" varieties)

GARLIC TIPS GALORE
On buying, storing, preparing, cooking, equivalents, and substitutes

BUYING FRESH GARLIC

Look for plump, firm garlic bulbs with dry, paperlike outer skins. If the skins are broken, or if the bulbs are soft, spongy, shriveled, or light for their size, walk away.

Because garlic is grown and harvested in different parts of the world, you'll find bulbs, or heads, available throughout the year. In the United States, the homegrown harvest is abundant during the summer and early fall and then starts to dwindle by winter. Although supermarkets keep their supplies fresh by importing garlic from other parts of the world, you need to be diligent in your selection. Properly harvested and cured softneck garlic will last up to 10 or 12 months; hardnecks can begin to show deterioration after 4 months.

One of garlic's culinary treats, reserved for the spring months of March to May, is **green garlic.** It has the look and texture of green onions but the subtle, distinctive flavor of garlic. Sliced, it's tasty when tossed in a salad, spring soup, or green garlic pesto. Your best bet for finding these exquisite plants is to shop at farmers' markets or specialty grocery stores that buy from local artisan farmers. While you're there, you might also discover **garlic chives** *(Allium tuberosum).* Popular in Chinese cuisine, they have a delicate garlic aroma and white chivelike flowers, and they make a lovely garnish.

A new and growing coterie of small artisan-style farms now offer garlic lovers a galaxy of exotic bulbs for eating as well as for growing their own brilliant array (it takes only a pot in a window or a plot in a sunny backyard). With access to the Internet and e-mail just a click away, a wonderful world of garlic is at our beck and call (see "Sources," page 126).

A word to the wise: Unless you're cooking something that requires large amounts of minced garlic, resist the temptation to buy already peeled or chopped garlic. You'll find that the flavor is harsher than that of fresh garlic, and when you store a jar in the refrigerator after opening it, chances are it will impart its distinctive flavor to other foods nearby.

STORING GARLIC

For best results, store your garlic in a cool, dry, airy place, such as a wire basket or garlic cellar (see "Garlic Gadgets and Gizmos," page 16). Avoid the refrigerator; its moist, cold atmosphere chills the flavor right out of garlic (this is true of the freezer as well). Depending on its variety and freshness when you buy it, garlic will keep for 4 to 10 months from the time of harvest. I buy and store only the amount I'm likely to use within 2 weeks. So forget about that emergency supply—a.k.a. the garlic braid that's adorned your kitchen wall for the last several years.

A word of warning: Some recipes call for you to store raw garlic in oil. There is a risk of botulism if you store the cloves at room temperature. Garlic preserved in oil is safe if it is refrigerated for up to 3 weeks, but after that, it should be discarded.

COOKING WITH GARLIC

One of the first things you realize about garlic is that it doesn't like to be peeled. Separating those pungent packets from their papery skins can be a problem. The easiest way to peel a clove is to first use a paring knife to remove the root end and the tip. Then peel or pull the skin away in sections. Another technique is to press the clove against a counter with the flat side of a heavy chef's knife and give it a press or a thump with your free hand. For dealing with larger quantities, look to the gadgets out there to help you (see "Garlic Gadgets and Gizmos," page 16), as well as to some old kitchen wisdom:

Clever cooks have learned that immersing cloves in hot water for 5 seconds (or in cold water for 20 minutes) loosens their skin. Slipping cloves into the microwave for 15 seconds also seems to do the trick.

CHOPPING OR MINCING garlic by hand, with the help of a good knife, brings out its best bright, deep flavors. It pays to have a high-carbon steel knife while prepping garlic for a recipe. When its hard surface comes into contact with the garlic's cell wall membranes, it releases less of the volatile sulfur-containing oils than a softer knife metal would. As I mentioned earlier, when a raw clove is chopped or crushed, an enzyme creates a reaction that causes garlic's characteristic odor. A sharp knife causes a smaller release of that enzyme. If you end up using the garlic in a cooked recipe, the harsh odor and taste disappear. For a whisper of garlic, keep the cloves whole or coarsely chopped, and add them at the beginning of cooking. For a shout, finely mince or press the cloves and add them toward the end of cooking.

For large quantities of chopped garlic, people frequently use their mini-prep or food processor. This may cut down on time, but it leaves the garlic unevenly cut and releases more juice and volatile oils, so the end product is more strongly flavored. If you do use a processor, chop the garlic in quick bursts.

MINCING OR CRUSHING GARLIC WITH SALT is a method many garlic-savvy cooks like to use. The salt absorbs the garlic juices and makes it easier to gather and remove the tiny garlic pieces. If chopped long enough, the mixture approaches the paste created by a mortar and pestle.

GRATING OR PRESSING GARLIC creates a mighty garlic presence when it is used raw. These two methods also create garlic pieces so small that they seem to melt and disappear in most recipes.

SAUTÉING GARLIC requires care and a watchful eye. It should be done slowly over low to medium heat in butter or oil. The setting depends on the individual stove, so you'll need to experiment. What you want in the end is to smell the fragrant garlic slowly cooking and to create soft, mellow pieces. If garlic burns or turns dark brown, it becomes bitter and can ruin a recipe.

ROASTING WHOLE GARLIC produces cloves that are creamy and have a nutty, caramel-like sweetness that is irresistible.

To roast a head of garlic, preheat the oven to 350°F. Slice off the top of the head to expose the tips of the cloves. Place the head, root side down, in a small ovenproof dish. Drizzle 1 tablespoon of olive oil over the exposed tips. (If desired, a teaspoon of water can also be added, and so can a sprinkling of salt.) Cover tightly with foil. Bake until tender and golden, about 1 hour. (At 325°F, bake it for about 1 1/4 hours.) Individual cloves can be roasted in the same manner but will take less time.

(Okay, so you're in a hurry, and you want your roasted garlic *fast*. To roast garlic in the microwave, place the prepared bulb on a paper towel. Microwave on high for 1 minute; turn the bulb upside down, and microwave for 1 more minute. You won't get the caramelly cloves or the wonderful aroma wafting through your house, but that's the price of being speedy.)

In Mexican cuisine, unpeeled garlic is roasted in an ungreased cast-iron skillet or griddle over medium heat. The cloves are stirred occasionally until blackened in spots and soft, about 15 minutes. Peeled and minced, they have a toasty flavor.

PICTURE-PERFECT GARLIC

Garlic's effect on a dish depends on how you prepare it. In this book, I use six different forms: rough paste, minced, chopped, crushed, sliced, and whole. This photograph shows what each form looks like before it is added to the recipe.

GARLIC GADGETS AND GIZMOS
Getting the groove on garlic

GARLIC CELLAR—A covered terra-cotta container with small, back-to-back holes in its side. It creates a dark, airy environment for keeping garlic fresh. You'll find garlic cellars in a variety of shapes and sizes. I think they really work.

GARLIC PEELER—A rubbery cylinder, like a cannoli shell, with a slightly sticky inside surface. It is designed to remove the clove's papery covering. Stick one or two garlic cloves inside, roll the cylinder back and forth, pressing down with your palm, and—presto!—out pops the naked clove. By the way, a rubber jar opener that you roll yourself also works.

GARLIC PRESS—A device that resembles a tiny lemon squeezer with teeth. It presses the garlic clove through small holes to extract the pulp and juice. Most sturdy presses don't require the cloves to be peeled, even though the instructions might say they do. Try it and see; if it works, you'll save yourself a lot of time.

GARLIC SLICER—Similar to a miniature mandoline, this gizmo cuts a clove into uniform, paper-thin slices. Some models have a reversible blade for finely shredding garlic.

GARLIC BAKER—Typically a small, round dish with a lip and a dome cover, this gadget takes the place of a foil-wrapped ramekin when you want to roast a whole garlic head. Kitschy designers have a field day with shapes and sizes.

ODOR BAR—A small, flat piece of ionized stainless steel created to remove garlic, onion, and fish odors from your hands. The magic happens when you rub your hands against the bar under cold running water. (Rumor has it that a stainless steel utensil or saucepan works just as well.)

FOR THE RECORD AND THE RECIPES

These equivalents are based on averages. If they differ slightly from yours, go ahead and scribble your results in this book so that you can refer to them whenever needed.

1 SMALL GARLIC HEAD =	1 1/2 TO 2 OUNCES =	10 OR LESS CLOVES
1 MEDIUM GARLIC HEAD =	2 TO 2 1/2 OUNCES =	10 CLOVES
1 LARGE GARLIC HEAD =	2 1/2 TO 3 OUNCES =	10 OR MORE CLOVES

1 MEDIUM GARLIC CLOVE, CHOPPED =	1 TO 1 1/4 TEASPOONS
1 MEDIUM GARLIC CLOVE, MINCED =	3/4 FIRMLY PACKED TEASPOON
1 MEDIUM GARLIC CLOVE, PRESSED =	1/2 TEASPOON

1 LARGE GARLIC CLOVE, CHOPPED =	2 FIRMLY PACKED TEASPOONS
1 LARGE GARLIC CLOVE, MINCED =	ABOUT 1 1/2 FIRMLY PACKED TEASPOONS
1 LARGE GARLIC CLOVE, PRESSED =	3/4 TO 1 TEASPOON

3 MEDIUM GARLIC CLOVES, THINLY SLICED BY HAND = 1 ROUNDED TABLESPOON

3 LARGE GARLIC CLOVES, SLICED BY HAND = 2 TABLESPOONS

3 LARGE GARLIC CLOVES, SLICED PAPER-THIN WITH A MANDOLINE = 2 TABLESPOONS

You can bring out more of garlic's potent flavor by pressing a single raw clove into the dish just before serving than you can by adding a giant handful at the beginning of a slow-cooked recipe.

FRESH OUT OF FRESH?

In a pinch, for 1 medium clove, substitute

A BIG PINCH OF GARLIC POWDER

1/4 TEASPOON GRANULATED GARLIC

1/2 TEASPOON GARLIC FLAKES

1/2 TEASPOON GARLIC SALT (AND REDUCE THE SALT IN YOUR RECIPE)

1 TEASPOON GARLIC JUICE

SPROUTING GREEN?

Ever notice the green center in a split clove? That sprout is the beginning of a new plant. It's not harmful, but it can be bitter. If you're going to eat the garlic raw, cut it out; otherwise, don't bother.

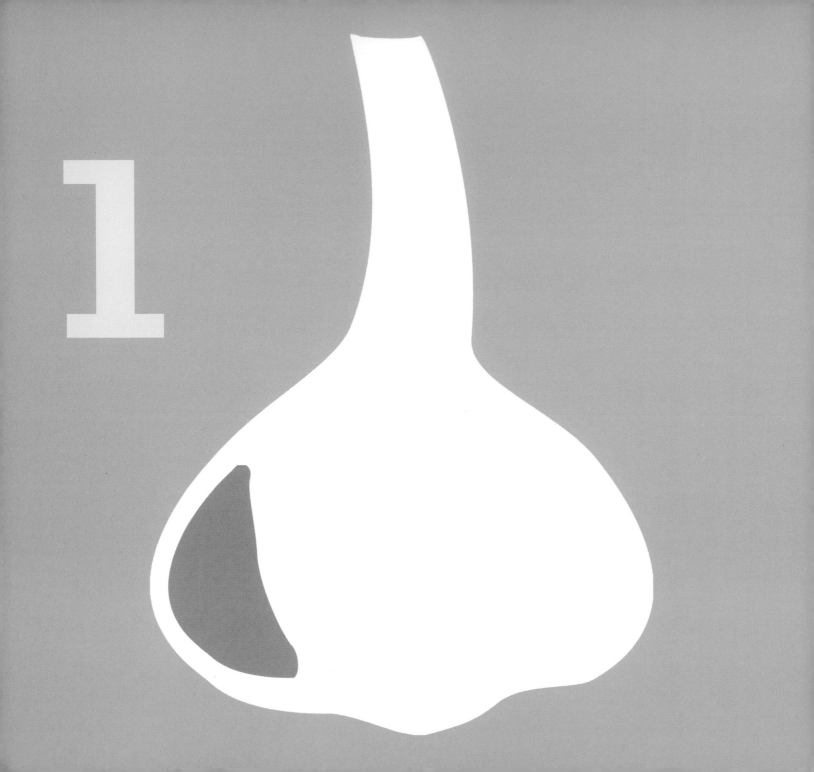

HIP DIPS, SMALL PLATES, AND LITTLE TEASERS

Little teasers with a kick and a whiff

CRUDITÉS WITH GARLIC GODDESS AND CURRIED GARLIC DIPS

Serves 6 to 8 (makes 1¼ cups of each dip)

Neither a haughty hors d'oeuvre nor a raid-the-refrigerator snack, these homemade garlic dips are marvelous little foods that make entertaining easy, especially when you serve them with your favorite crudités from the list below. Garlic is the star ingredient in both dips. But the Garlic Goddess Dip is enlivened by fresh tarragon, parsley, and lemon juice, while the Curried Garlic Dip, made with tangy yogurt, gets an exotic blitz from curry and ginger. + For the curried dip, you need to first turn the yogurt into a thick, soft yogurt cheese by leaving it overnight to drain in a sieve, so plan accordingly.

GARLIC GODDESS DIP

2 LARGE GARLIC CLOVES, MINCED (1 FIRMLY
   PACKED TABLESPOON)
½ CUP COARSELY CHOPPED FLAT-LEAF
   PARSLEY
1 TABLESPOON MINCED FRESH TARRAGON
1 TEASPOON ANCHOVY PASTE
2 TABLESPOONS FRESH LEMON JUICE
½ CUP MAYONNAISE
½ CUP SOUR CREAM
COARSE SALT, PREFERABLY KOSHER, AND
   FRESHLY GROUND PEPPER

CURRIED GARLIC DIP

2 CUPS PLAIN WHOLE-MILK YOGURT
2 PACKAGES (3 OUNCES EACH) CREAM
   CHEESE, AT ROOM TEMPERATURE
2 TEASPOONS HONEY, AT ROOM
   TEMPERATURE OR LUKEWARM
2 OR 3 MEDIUM GARLIC CLOVES, DIVIDED
1 TEASPOON CURRY POWDER
¼ TEASPOON GROUND GINGER
1 TABLESPOON FRESH LIME JUICE

CRUDITÉS AND THE GREAT DIPPERS
   (SEE SIDEBAR)

FOR THE GARLIC GODDESS DIP: In a mini-prep processor, combine the garlic, parsley, and tarragon and process until finely minced. Add the anchovy paste and lemon juice and process until blended. Transfer to a small bowl and stir in the mayonnaise and sour cream until blended. Taste and adjust the seasoning with salt and pepper. Refrigerate until serving time.

FOR THE CURRIED GARLIC DIP: In a fine-mesh sieve placed over a bowl, drain the yogurt overnight. Discard the liquid and transfer the yogurt to a medium bowl.

In the bowl, mix together the yogurt, cream cheese, and honey until smooth. Press 2 of the garlic cloves, and stir into the mixture; add the curry powder, ground ginger, and lime juice. Refrigerate until serving time. Taste before serving. For more garlic flavor, press another clove and stir it in.

CRUDITÉS AND THE GREAT DIPPERS

ARTICHOKES, STEAMED	CHERRY TOMATOES	SNOW PEAS
ASPARAGUS, STEAMED	CHINESE CABBAGE STRIPS	SPINACH LEAVES
BABY NEW POTATOES,	CUCUMBER STRIPS	BAGEL CHIPS
STEAMED	ENDIVE LEAVES	BREADSTICKS
BELL PEPPER STRIPS, RED,	FENNEL SLICES	CHICKEN CHUNKS OR STRIPS
GREEN, ORANGE, YELLOW,	JICAMA SLICES OR STICKS	ROAST BEEF CHUNKS
OR PURPLE	MUSHROOMS	SALAMI, SLICED OR CUBED
BROCCOLI FLORETS	PEA PODS	SHRIMP, COOKED
CARROT STRIPS	RED RADISHES, WHITE OR	
CAULIFLOWER FLORETS	BLACK DAIKON	
CELERY STRIPS	INNER ROMAINE LEAVES	

HAPPY HOUR BAR NUTS

Makes 4 cups

This fragrant combination of warm walnuts, pecans, garlic, and rosemary has such great taste and personality that it can arrive solo at your next cocktail gathering or mingle merrily with other hors d'oeuvres. It makes any hour happier. But beware: If you put these treats out too early, you'll be sorry because no one (hosts included) can eat just one. They're savory, yet slightly sweet, and salty, with plenty of garlicky bite.

2 TABLESPOONS UNSALTED BUTTER

6 MEDIUM GARLIC CLOVES, MINCED
(4 1/2 FIRMLY PACKED TEASPOONS)

1/4 CUP PLUS 2 TABLESPOONS FIRMLY
PACKED LIGHT BROWN SUGAR

1 TABLESPOON WATER

1 TABLESPOON FINELY MINCED FRESH
ROSEMARY

2 TEASPOONS GARLIC SALT, PLUS MORE
FOR SPRINKLING

2 CUPS WALNUT HALVES (7 1/2 OUNCES)

2 CUPS PECAN HALVES (7 1/2 OUNCES)

Preheat the oven to 350°F.

In a large saucepan, melt the butter over medium heat. Add the garlic and sauté for 1 minute. Add the brown sugar, water, rosemary, and garlic salt and sauté, stirring constantly, until the sugar is no longer dry and the mixture is shiny and wet. Add the nuts and toss to coat.

Line a rimmed baking sheet with foil or parchment paper, and spread the nuts in a single layer. Bake for 8 minutes. Remove and toss the nuts on the baking sheet to coat again. Return to the oven and bake until lightly browned, about 6 minutes. Remove and immediately sprinkle the nuts with garlic salt, then toss again, scooping up any coating left on the foil. Slide the foil onto a wire rack and allow the nuts to cool completely. Store in an airtight container.

EDAMAME WITH PEPPERCORN GARLIC SALT

Serves 4 (makes about 4 cups)

Roasted edamame are among the simplest new hors d'oeuvres to hit the cocktail circuit. Isn't it great when a vegetable that's good for you can also be easy to fix, tasty, and fun to eat? Once the pods are tossed with the pepper-seasoned garlic salt and briefly roasted, you get to split the pods and pop the beans right into your mouth, over and over again. That's what I did the first time I tried a rendition of this recipe at Saucebox, a savvy, hip haven of eating in Portland, Oregon.

1 1/2 TEASPOONS WHOLE PEPPERCORNS, SUCH AS WHITE, SZECHWAN, OR RAINBOW BLEND

2 1/2 TEASPOONS GARLIC SALT

1 POUND FRESH OR FROZEN AND THAWED SOYBEANS (EDAMAME) IN THEIR PODS

Preheat the oven to 450°F.

In a small skillet, toast the peppercorns over medium-low heat until fragrant, about 5 minutes. Remove from the heat and transfer to a blender, mortar and pestle, or spice grinder (or a propeller-style coffee grinder, wiped clean before and after use). Add the garlic salt and grind the peppercorns to a coarse powder. To remove any peppercorn husks, pass through a fine sieve. Set aside.

On a rimmed baking sheet, spread the soybeans in a single layer. Sprinkle the garlic salt mixture over the pods and toss to coat. Roast until tender, 5 to 7 minutes. Serve warm.

VARIATION:

In a hurry? Next time you're at a specialty supermarket, gourmet shop, or ethnic grocery store, purchase a jar or tin of an interesting spice or pepper mix. Then just measure and mix it with the salt and you're ready to sprinkle it. My favorite is shichimi, a peppery Japanese spice mix made from seven different seasonings, including red chili flakes, dried mandarin orange peel, and white poppy seeds.

ROASTED GARLIC AND WHITE BEAN SPREAD

Serves 4 (makes about 1¹/₂ cups)

Many years ago, my husband, Pete, who likes good food as much as I do, took me to a cozy Italian café, Three Doors Down, in Portland, Oregon. Everything we tasted was superb, including the garlic-laced white bean spread we luxuriously slathered on our bread before dinner. Here's my rendition of this memorable dish with the sweet, mellow flavor of roasted garlic. The subtle combination of roasted garlic and creamy white beans is delicious in itself. But it takes on an especially beguiling personality when it's drizzled with a lemony vinaigrette.

SPREAD

CLOVES FROM 2 MEDIUM HEADS
   ROASTED GARLIC (2 TO 2¹/₂ OUNCES
   EACH RAW) (SEE PAGE 14)

1 CAN (15 OUNCES) WHITE BEANS,
   DRAINED AND RINSED (ABOUT
   1¹/₂ CUPS)

¹/₂ TEASPOON OR MORE COARSE SALT,
   PREFERABLY KOSHER

EXTRA-VIRGIN OLIVE OIL FOR THINNING
   (OPTIONAL)

VINAIGRETTE

2 TABLESPOONS EXTRA-VIRGIN
   OLIVE OIL

1 TABLESPOON FRESH LEMON JUICE

¹/₄ TEASPOON DIJON MUSTARD

SLICED BAGUETTE, TOASTED PITA BREAD
   WEDGES, OR CRUSTY ITALIAN BREAD
   FOR SERVING

TO MAKE THE SPREAD: Squeeze the soft, golden cloves out of their skins into the bowl of a food processor. Use the back of a spoon to mash the cloves against the side of the bowl. Add the beans and salt and process until the mixture is smooth and holds its shape. (If the mixture is too thick, stir in a little olive oil.) Taste and adjust the seasoning with salt, if desired.

TO MAKE THE VINAIGRETTE: In a small bowl or cup, whisk together the olive oil, lemon juice, and mustard.

To serve, mound the spread on a plate and drizzle with vinaigrette. Serve with sliced baguette, toasted pita bread wedges, or crusty Italian bread.

BAGNA CAUDA

Serves 4 to 6 (makes about 3 cups dip)

"It's Italian fondue," Pat Raschio explains as the whole Raschio clan gathers to celebrate his birthday. With dozens of relatives packing the living and dining rooms, the furniture heads for the walls. In the kitchen his wife, Diane, ladles the warm, garlicky dip into fondue pots and chafing dishes as long lines of folding tables are loaded with platters of crudités and crusty breads. + As the eating begins, one hand dips and lifts the vegetables from chafing dish to mouth, while the other hand holds a piece of bread underneath to catch the drips. After a few round-trips, the "napkin" bread is divinely soggy and ready to be devoured. After two hours, the garlicky dip is nearly gone, but what remains is thick, spreadable, and even more heavenly. The last person standing (and dipping) is declared the winner, and another bottle of Chianti is opened.

3/4 CUP MINCED GARLIC (ABOUT
    24 LARGE CLOVES) (SEE NOTE)
2 CUPS EXTRA-VIRGIN OLIVE OIL,
    DIVIDED
2 CANS (2 OUNCES EACH) ANCHOVY
    FILLETS, RINSED, DRAINED, AND
    CHOPPED
1/2 CUP (1 STICK) UNSALTED BUTTER
1 TO 2 TEASPOONS COARSE SALT,
    PREFERABLY KOSHER
ASSORTED CRUDITÉS (PAGE 20)
    (SEE NOTE)
CHUNKS OF RUSTIC BREAD

In a 10- to 12-inch, medium-heavy saucepan, sauté the garlic in 1/3 cup of the oil over medium heat until fragrant, 1 to 2 minutes. Do not let brown. Add the anchovies, stirring frequently with a wooden spoon until the fillets dissolve. Add the butter and the remaining 1 2/3 cups oil and heat until the butter melts and the mixture is moderately hot. Stir in 1 teaspoon salt, taste, and adjust the seasoning with more salt if needed. Carefully transfer to a chafing dish over hot water or to a ceramic fondue pot over a low alcohol flame. (Remember to keep the heat at a minimum, no greater than candle intensity.) Serve with assorted crudités and chunks of rustic bread.

NOTE: For this much minced garlic, there are those who swear by the convenience of already-minced garlic that you can purchase in jars at the supermarket.

Vegetable dippers can be prepared a day ahead and kept in the refrigerator, covered with cold water. You can also arrange them on a clean, damp kitchen towel and store them in a resealable plastic bag. (I often stack several layers in a single bag.)

ARTICHOKES WITH GARLICKY AÏOLI

Serves 2 (makes 1 scant cup aïoli)

The early Romans and Greeks, and the Syrians before them, knew that artichokes were the best of all finger foods. We know it too: We use them as appetizers; we use them as a first course; we even take the hearts out and toss them in a salad. I consider an artichoke my own private crudité cache. Could it be that the artichoke is just a vehicle for delivering another delicious taste of garlic? + When preparing aïoli, or any mayonnaise, it is important to have all the ingredients at room temperature. Then, when you slowly add the olive oil, you'll get a rich and creamy emulsion.

2 ARTICHOKES (ABOUT 10 OUNCES EACH)

AÏOLI

4 LARGE GARLIC CLOVES, CUT IN HALF

1/2 TEASPOON COARSE SALT, PREFERABLY
  KOSHER

2 EGG YOLKS, AT ROOM TEMPERATURE
  (SEE NOTE)

1/4 TO 1/2 TEASPOON DIJON MUSTARD

PINCH OF GROUND PEPPER, PREFERABLY
  WHITE

2 TABLESPOONS FRESH LEMON JUICE,
  AT ROOM TEMPERATURE

3/4 CUP EXTRA-VIRGIN OLIVE OIL OR
  CANOLA OIL OR A COMBINATION, AT
  ROOM TEMPERATURE, DIVIDED

VARIATION:

For **PEPPERY GARLIC AÏOLI,** follow the aïoli recipe, substituting 1/4 to 1/2 teaspoon cayenne pepper for the ground pepper.

TO PREPARE THE ARTICHOKES: Remove the loose outer leaves of the artichokes and trim the stems even with the bottoms so they sit upright. Cut 1 inch off of the tops. (If desired, you can snip off the sharp leaf tips and brush the edges with lemon juice to prevent browning.)

In a large pot, cover and cook the artichokes in boiling salted water until a leaf pulls out easily, 20 to 30 minutes. Turn upside down and drain well.

TO PREPARE THE AÏOLI: Sprinkle the garlic with the salt and mince, pressing the garlic into the salt with the flat of the knife to form a rough paste. Transfer to the bowl of a food processor or blender. Add the egg yolks, mustard, pepper, lemon juice, and 1/4 cup of the oil. Turn on the processor and add the remaining 1/2 cup oil in a thin stream. (If the mixture is too thick, with the machine running, add 1 or 2 teaspoons of oil or warm water.) Taste, adjust the seasoning, and serve. Refrigerate any leftover aïoli in a covered container for up to 5 days.

To serve, turn the artichokes right side up and accompany them with a small dish of aïoli.

NOTE: To bring a chilled egg to room temperature, immerse the whole egg in a small bowl of warm water for 10 minutes.

SAFETY TIP: Since this mayonnaise contains raw egg, it is important to use the freshest eggs possible, free of cracks and kept refrigerated. Because raw eggs carry the risk of bacteria that can cause salmonella poisoning, they should not be served to high-risk groups, such as the elderly, very young, chronically ill, and pregnant women. Pasteurized eggs, which undergo the same process as milk to destroy harmful bacteria, are available at speciality supermarkets.

SAVORY GARLIC POLENTA ROUNDS

Makes about 15 rounds

These bite-size, mellow garlic polenta rounds vanish as soon as they're spotted. Served slightly warm and unadorned, they're a welcoming prelude to dinner. Guests love their taste. They also love the fact that they're not filling up on rich, highly flavored appetizers, which often spoil the delight of the main meal. If you want a more substantial *amuse-bouche,* add a dollop of Golden Garlic, Onion, and Shallot Marmalade (page 116), mild goat cheese, or slivers of olives, salami, and roasted red pepper.

1/4 CUP HEAVY (WHIPPING) CREAM

3 LARGE GARLIC CLOVES, PRESSED

2 CUPS WATER

1 TEASPOON SALT

2/3 CUP QUICK-COOKING POLENTA

1 TABLESPOON UNSALTED BUTTER

COARSE SALT, PREFERABLY KOSHER, AND
   FRESHLY GROUND PEPPER

In a small saucepan, combine the cream and garlic over medium-high heat and bring to a simmer. Remove from the heat and let steep for 5 to 7 minutes. Strain the cream, discarding the garlic.

In a heavy saucepan, combine the water and salt over medium-high heat and bring to a boil. Add the polenta in a slow, steady stream, whisking constantly. Reduce the heat to a simmer and cook until the polenta thickens and begins to pull away from the sides of the pan, about 4 minutes. Stir the cream and butter into the polenta, whisking constantly, and cook for 1 to 2 minutes. Remove from the heat. Taste and adjust the seasoning with salt and pepper to taste.

On a baking sheet, spread the polenta into a 6-by-9-inch rectangle about 1/2 inch thick. Allow to cool completely.

Preheat the oven to 350°F.

Using a 1 1/2-inch round garnish cutter, cut the polenta into rounds and transfer to an ungreased or parchment-lined baking sheet. Bake until hot but not brown, about 10 minutes. Serve warm. (You also can use a larger biscuit cutter to make the rounds and then cut each round into 4 wedges.)

BETTY'S WARM GARLIC MUSHROOMS ON GRILLED COUNTRY BREAD

Serves 8

I'm crazy about these warm, garlic-scented mushrooms made by my friend and fellow cookbook author Betty Rosbottom. Quickly sautéed and seasoned with a flavorful garlic butter, they're used here to top toasted French bread slices as a small plate or a little teaser before the main event. But don't be surprised if you find yourself making them when there's no one around to cook for but your lonesome. These mushrooms are addictive.

3 1/2 TABLESPOONS UNSALTED BUTTER,
    AT ROOM TEMPERATURE
3 LARGE GARLIC CLOVES, MINCED
    (1 FIRMLY PACKED TABLESPOON)
2 TEASPOONS FINELY CHOPPED SHALLOT
3 TABLESPOONS CHOPPED FLAT-LEAF
    PARSLEY, DIVIDED
1/2 TEASPOON COARSE SALT, PREFERABLY
    KOSHER
FRESHLY GROUND PEPPER
8 OUNCES WHITE MUSHROOMS
2 OUNCES FRESH SHIITAKES, GIROLLES, OR
    CHANTERELLES, OR A COMBINATION
OLIVE OIL FOR SAUTÉING MUSHROOMS
8 TO 10 SLICES CRUSTY FRENCH BREAD,
    1/4 TO 1/2 INCH THICK, LIGHTLY
    TOASTED OR GRILLED AND BRUSHED
    WITH OLIVE OIL

In a small mixing bowl, blend together the butter, garlic, shallot, 1 1/2 tablespoons of the parsley, salt, and pepper. If not using immediately, cover with plastic wrap and refrigerate. (The seasoned butter can be prepared a day ahead; bring to room temperature before using.)

Using a clean, damp cloth, remove any dirt from the mushrooms by wiping all the surfaces. Halve the mushrooms through the stems, then cut each half in 1/2-inch slices, and set aside. (For shiitakes, remove tough stems and discard. Leave smaller mushrooms whole or halve them through the stems.) Using a large, heavy skillet, add enough olive oil to lightly coat the bottom of the pan over medium-high heat. When the oil is hot, add the mushrooms and cook, stirring only occasionally, until browned. If necessary, add a little extra oil to keep the mushrooms from burning. The mushrooms will exude juices while cooking. Continue to cook until all the liquid has evaporated. The total cooking time should be about 5 minutes. When the mushrooms are browned and no liquid remains, add the garlic butter mixture and stir until melted. Taste and adjust the seasoning with salt and pepper. (The mushrooms can be prepared several hours ahead. Leave at room temperature and reheat until hot when ready to serve.) To serve, mound the mushrooms on toasted bread slices. Generously sprinkle each serving with some of the remaining 1 1/2 tablespoons parsley. Serve hot.

SKORDALIA WITH PITA BREAD WEDGES

Serves 4 to 6 (makes 2 cups)

The Greek moon was nearly full as three colleagues and I followed the young girls down the curving dirt road to Maria Meimetea's house in the southern peninsular village of Stouppa. On one side, the hillside gave way to the Aegean and a stone beach where Zorba once danced. Maria's daughter and niece had been sent to the main road to fetch the four American journalists and their interpreter for an evening of cooking and eating—the best sort of foreign diplomacy. + While Maria helped one of us roll out pastry on her dining room table for a savory spinach pie, I was in the galley kitchen with her sister Tassia, putting the finishing touches on several antipasto dishes, including skordalia, a light-textured, delicious Greek dip of garlic, bread, potatoes, and almonds, flavored with olive oil and lemon juice. I loved it. + When the skordalia was ready to enjoy and the spinach pie was baking, the table was wiped and brought to the center of the room. Chairs and people were gathered for a several-hour feast. In between courses, I tried to write down the recipes' instructions, given to me with pointed fingers, waving gestures, and lots and lots of laughter. With a few concessions to American ingredients, I think I've succeeded in making a dish Maria would love as much as I do.

1 POTATO (8 OUNCES), SUCH AS YUKON
   GOLD OR RED BLISS
2 CUPS FRESH BREAD CUBES, CUT FROM
   A FINE-GRAINED RUSTIC BREAD
   (3/4-INCH CUBES)
4 TO 6 MEDIUM GARLIC CLOVES, CHOPPED
   (1 TO 1 1/2 FIRMLY PACKED TEASPOONS)
1/3 CUP BLANCHED OR LIGHTLY TOASTED
   WHOLE ALMONDS, CHOPPED
1/3 CUP EXTRA-VIRGIN OLIVE OIL
3 1/2 TABLESPOONS FRESH LEMON JUICE
ABOUT 1/4 CUP WARM WATER
COARSE SALT, PREFERABLY KOSHER, AND
   FRESHLY GROUND PEPPER
CAPER BRINE OR WHITE WINE VINEGAR
   FOR SEASONING
PITA BREAD ROUNDS, CUT INTO WEDGES,
   FOR SERVING

In a saucepan over medium-high heat, cover the potato with water and bring to a boil. Cook until the potato is tender, 20 to 25 minutes. When the potato is cool enough to handle, peel, mash, and set aside.

In a medium bowl, soak the bread cubes in water to cover until softened. Squeeze out the excess water and transfer to the bowl of a food processor. Add the garlic and almonds and process into a smooth paste. With the motor running, add the oil, a little at a time, followed by the lemon juice. Process until combined.

Scrape into a medium bowl and fold in the mashed potato. Blend in the warm water until the mixture is the desired consistency. Season to taste with salt and pepper. Taste and adjust the seasoning with caper brine. Cover and refrigerate for at least 4 hours or overnight to let the flavors blend. Bring to room temperature to serve with pita bread wedges.

CREMINI CAPS STUFFED WITH GARLIC, CHEESE, AND SMOKED HAM

Makes 12 stuffed mushrooms

Just when you thought stuffed mushrooms were old-fashioned and their fillings uninspired, along come these luscious and lusty morsels. When combined with smoky ham, fresh parsley, and tangy, soft Italian cheese, the pressed, pungent garlic makes a delectable filling. I often serve these mushrooms as a first course before grilled steaks or lamb chops, but they would be equally good with a vegetarian pasta dish.

12 MEDIUM CREMINI OR PORCINI MUSH-
ROOMS, 2 1/2 INCHES IN DIAMETER

2 TABLESPOONS EXTRA-VIRGIN OLIVE
OIL

4 MEDIUM GARLIC CLOVES, PRESSED

1/3 CUP MINCED FRESH PARSLEY, PLUS
MORE FOR GARNISHING (GARNISH
OPTIONAL)

1/2 CUP (2 OUNCES) FINELY CHOPPED
COOKED BONELESS SMOKED HAM,
PORK CHOP, OR CANADIAN BACON,
RIND REMOVED (SEE NOTE)

2 TABLESPOONS FINELY CRUSHED HOME-
MADE (PAGE 62) OR PURCHASED
GARLIC CROUTONS OR BREAD CRUMBS

COARSE SALT, PREFERABLY KOSHER

3 OUNCES CHILLED ASIAGO FRESCO,
RIND REMOVED AND CHEESE GRATED
(SEE NOTE)

Preheat the oven to 375°F.

Wipe the mushrooms clean and pull out the stems, leaving the caps whole. Transfer the caps to a baking pan large enough to hold all the caps in one layer. Mince the stems, and set aside.

In a medium sauté pan, heat the olive oil over medium heat. Add the garlic, parsley, ham, bread crumbs, and mushroom stems. Sauté, stirring constantly, until the garlic is fragrant and the bread crumbs are softened, about 5 minutes. Remove from the heat, season to taste with salt, and transfer to a medium bowl to cool slightly. Add the cheese and toss to combine.

Fill each mushroom cap with enough cheese mixture to form a small mound covering the entire cap. Bake until the cheese melts and the mushrooms soften, about 20 minutes. Garnish with additional parsley, if desired, and serve immediately.

NOTE: Many supermarket meat or deli departments carry packaged sliced boneless smoked ham, pork chops, and Canadian bacon.

If Asiago fresco is unavailable, consider Taleggio, another semisoft Italian cheese with a sweet, tangy flavor.

GRILLED SHRIMP WITH TOMATILLO-GARLIC SALSA

Serves 3 or 4

This is one of my favorite outdoor party foods, and guests seem to agree. No matter what else I'm serving, the zesty, garlic-dusted grilled shrimp are eaten first, but not before they're dipped and tipped with the spicy tomatillo-garlic salsa. The colorful combination of rosy shrimp and green salsa also makes this an eye-catching first course. I like to divide it into individual servings and garnish with crumbly *queso fresco*. + Colorful green salsas using fresh tomatillos, garlic, jalapeño pepper, and cilantro are popular in Mexico. *Salsa verde* enlivens all kinds of great everyday dishes, and good, fresh garlic (especially the red-skinned hardneck variety found in the summertime) is fundamental to every rendition. This is the version I like, but go ahead and experiment with your own proportions; just keep the garlic in good supply.

SALSA

7 MEDIUM FRESH TOMATILLOS, HUSKED
   AND STEMMED (SEE NOTE)

4 LARGE GARLIC CLOVES, CUT IN HALF

1/2 TEASPOON KOSHER SALT

1 SMALL TO MEDIUM JALAPEÑO PEPPER,
   SEEDED AND COARSELY CHOPPED

1/3 CUP CHOPPED ONION

1/3 CUP LOOSELY PACKED FRESH CILANTRO
   LEAVES, COARSELY CHOPPED

1/2 TEASPOON GROUND CUMIN

1 TEASPOON FRESH LIME JUICE, OR TO TASTE

2 MEDIUM GARLIC CLOVES, THINLY SLICED

SHRIMP

12 TO 16 JUMBO SHRIMP, PEELED AND
   DEVEINED, WITH TAILS LEFT INTACT

3 TABLESPOONS OLIVE OIL

1 TABLESPOON MILD CHILI POWDER

1 TABLESPOON GARLIC POWDER

COARSE SALT, PREFERABLY KOSHER, AND
   FRESHLY GROUND PEPPER

1/3 CUP CRUMBLED QUESO FRESCO OR FETA
   CHEESE (OPTIONAL)

TO MAKE THE SALSA: In a medium pot of boiling salted water, cook the tomatillos for 4 minutes. Drain and set aside to cool.

Meanwhile, sprinkle the halved garlic with the salt and mince, pressing the garlic into the salt with the flat of the knife to form a rough paste. Transfer to a blender and add the jalapeño, onion, cilantro, cumin, and 1 teaspoon lime juice. Coarsely chop the tomatillos and transfer to the blender. Process until blended; you should still see small chunky pieces. Transfer to a bowl and remove any large slivers of tomatillo skin. Set aside to cool, or cover and refrigerate until ready to use. Taste and adjust the seasoning with lime juice. (The salsa can be made up to 3 days ahead.) Add the sliced garlic and toss 30 minutes before serving.

TO PREPARE THE SHRIMP: Light a medium-high fire in a charcoal or gas grill. Arrange the shrimp in a baking dish, drizzle with the olive oil, and toss to coat. In a small bowl, mix together the chili powder and garlic powder. Sprinkle the shrimp with half of this mixture. Turn the shrimp over and sprinkle with the remaining chili powder mixture. Grill the shrimp until just cooked, about 2 minutes per side. Remove and sprinkle with salt and pepper to taste.

To serve, spoon about 3 tablespoons of the tomatillo salsa in the center of a small plate. Arrange 4 shrimp on top. Sprinkle with *queso fresco,* if desired, and serve.

NOTE: A member of the gooseberry family, tomatillo has a papery husk that needs to be peeled before using. Look for ones that have a yellowish tinge and are slightly soft.

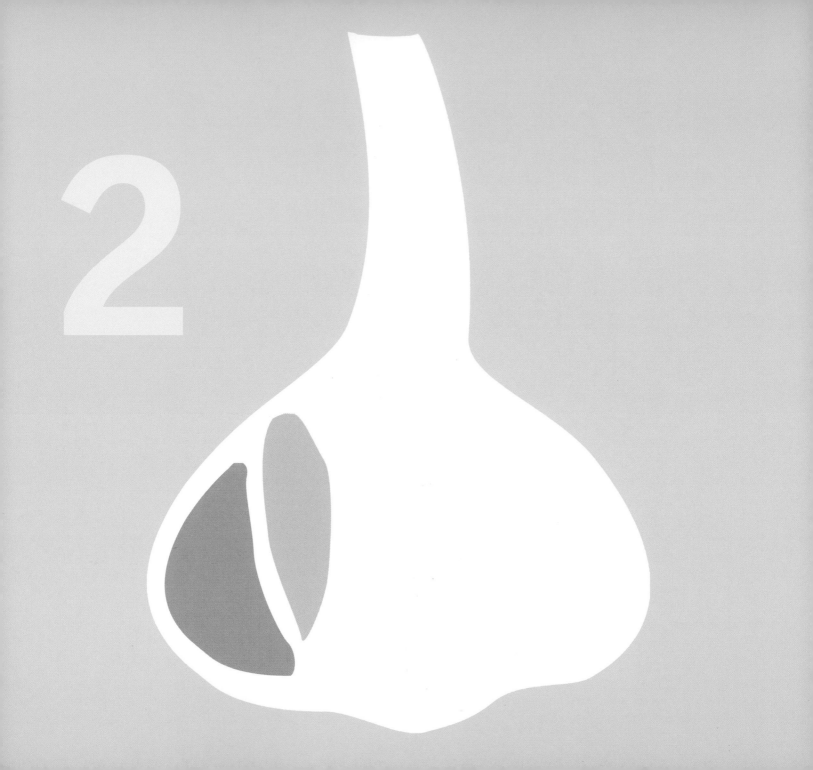

SOUPS AND SALADS

Savory sips and crispy greens scented with garlic

GARLIC BROTH

Makes about 6 cups

Use this broth as a base for other soups or for creations of your own with leftover diced tomatoes, cooked peas, cilantro, basil, lime zest, or other favorites.

2 LARGE HEADS GARLIC (2^1/$_2$ TO
   3 OUNCES EACH), CLOVES SEPARATED
   AND PEELED

6 CUPS WATER

1 TABLESPOON EXTRA-VIRGIN OLIVE OIL

3 SPRIGS THYME

5 SPRIGS FLAT-LEAF PARSLEY

8 PEPPERCORNS

2 TEASPOONS COARSE SALT, PREFERABLY
   KOSHER, OR MORE TO TASTE

In a large pot, combine the garlic, water, olive oil, thyme, parsley, peppercorns, and salt over medium-high heat and bring to a boil. Reduce the heat to a simmer, cover, and cook for 1^1/$_2$ hours. Strain out the garlic and herbs and discard. Taste, and adjust the seasoning with salt. (The broth can be made up to 4 days ahead. Cool, cover, and refrigerate, or freeze for up to 3 months.)

"LET'S FEEL BETTER" BROTH

Serves 4 (makes about 5$\frac{1}{2}$ cups)

This started out as a soup my friend and fellow cook Jane Zwinger concocted to help us both feel better during a long siege of bad colds. We needed something zesty to bolster our moods (and clear our sinuses) and something quick to make with ingredients readily at hand. This tangy broth did the trick (especially when we upped the amount of Tabasco). In fact, it tastes so good, we continue to enjoy it as an afternoon pick-me-up. + We chose ingredients not only for their flavor, but for their curative and nourishing powers as well. Garlic has antibiotic properties and is useful in clearing respiratory illnesses. Ginger and Tabasco sauce are warming and work as expectorants. Chicken broth contains drug-like agents similar to those found in modern cold medicines (No wonder it was first prescribed as a cold remedy in the twelfth century.) Tomatoes, orange juice, and carrots contain vitamins C and A, which boost the immune system. Simmered together, these taste mighty good when you're trying to ease the sniffles, coughs, and fevers of a cold.

2 CANS (14$\frac{1}{2}$ OUNCES EACH) CHICKEN
   BROTH

1 CAN (14$\frac{1}{2}$ OUNCES) DICED TOMATOES
   WITH JUICE

1 TABLESPOON THINLY SLICED GARLIC
   (3 TO 4 MEDIUM CLOVES)

2 MEDIUM GARLIC CLOVES, PRESSED, OR
   MORE TO TASTE

1 MEDIUM CARROT, PEELED AND GRATED

ONE 1$\frac{1}{2}$-INCH PIECE ($\frac{3}{4}$ OUNCE) FRESH
   GINGER, PEELED, CUT LENGTHWISE INTO
   6 THIN SLICES, AND JULIENNED

$\frac{1}{4}$ CUP ORANGE JUICE

1 TABLESPOON FRESH LIME JUICE

$\frac{1}{8}$ TO $\frac{1}{4}$ TEASPOON TABASCO SAUCE,
   OR MORE TO TASTE

$\frac{1}{2}$ TEASPOON COARSE SALT, PREFERABLY
   KOSHER, OR MORE TO TASTE

2 TEASPOONS SUGAR (OPTIONAL)

In a large saucepan, combine the chicken broth, tomatoes with juice, sliced garlic, pressed garlic, carrot, and ginger over medium-high heat and bring to a boil. Reduce the heat and simmer for 10 minutes. Stir in the orange juice, lime juice, and Tabasco, beginning with $\frac{1}{8}$ teaspoon and adding more to taste. Cover and let steep for 30 minutes. Taste and adjust the seasoning with the salt, sugar, and Tabasco.

VARIATION:

For added nourishment, feel free to add a little cooked chicken and perhaps some petite green peas for color. It all adds up to good taste.

MY OREGON BOUILLABAISSE WITH PEPPERY GARLIC AÏOLI CROUTONS

Serves 4 to 6 (makes about 6¹/₂ cups)

The Oregon coast may not boast the sandy beaches and décolletage found along the French Mediterranean coast, but it certainly has delicious seafood and the right to its own lusty version of this classic fish soup. In Marseilles, I know, shellfish are not part of the tradition. But in the Pacific Northwest, we love shrimp and prize our mussels. Along with these unconventional ingredients, those who want an extra gust of garlic can include the soft, golden whole cloves from two roasted garlic heads when adding the wine. + In this recipe, the Peppery Garlic Aïoli Croutons are akin to bruschetta. They can be enjoyed on top of the soup or served on the side for people to add as they want.

2 TABLESPOONS OLIVE OIL

4 TO 5 LARGE GARLIC CLOVES, MINCED
    (ABOUT 2 FIRMLY PACKED TABLESPOONS)

1 CAN (28 OUNCES) DICED TOMATOES
    WITH JUICE

1 CUP CLAM JUICE

1 CUP CHARDONNAY OR DRY VERMOUTH

¹/₂ TEASPOON GRATED ORANGE ZEST

¹/₈ TEASPOON FENNEL SEEDS, CRUSHED

PINCH OF SAFFRON THREADS

COARSE SALT, PREFERABLY KOSHER, AND
    FRESHLY GROUND PEPPER

6 TO 8 OUNCES SALMON FILLET, TRIMMED
    OF SKIN AND BONES AND CUT INTO
    1-INCH CUBES

6 TO 8 OUNCES HALIBUT CHEEKS, CUT
    INTO 1-INCH CUBES

12 MEDIUM SHRIMP, PEELED AND DEVEINED

12 MUSSELS, SCRUBBED, WITH BEARDS
    REMOVED

PEPPERY GARLIC AÏOLI (PAGE 27)

1 FRENCH BREAD BAGUETTE, CUT IN
    ¹/₃-INCH-THICK SLICES AND TOASTED

CHOPPED FRESH PARSLEY FOR GARNISHING

In a 6-quart Dutch oven or soup pot, heat the olive oil over medium heat. Add the garlic and sauté until fragrant, 1 to 2 minutes. Do not let it brown. Stir in the tomatoes with juice, clam juice, wine, orange zest, fennel seeds, and saffron. Bring to a boil over medium heat. Reduce the heat to a simmer and cook for 30 minutes. Taste and adjust the seasoning with salt and pepper.

Add the salmon and halibut and simmer for 5 minutes. (Keep the simmer gentle so that the seafood does not toughen.) Add the shrimp and mussels and cook until the mussels are open and the shrimp are pink, about 2 minutes. (Discard any mussels that failed to open.)

To serve, ladle the soup into large, shallow bowls. Spread or dollop some aïoli over each piece of toast. Top each serving of soup with 2 toasts, sprinkle with parsley, and serve. At the table, serve the additional toast, if desired.

GARLIC, LEEK, AND POTATO SOUP WITH WHIPPED GARLIC CREAM

Serves 6 (makes about 7 cups)

Three earthy vegetables—garlic, leek, and potato—combine to create a savory, satisfying soup that can be served hot, chilled, or at room temperature. The garlic-infused broth establishes an undertone that perfumes the entire dish, and the heady aroma culminates in the Whipped Garlic Cream garnish, a refined finish for any cream-based soup. + When puréeing this soup (or any hot liquid) in a blender, be sure the lid is firmly attached, and remove the small plastic insert from the lid. This allows steam to escape. Also, to avoid getting splattered with the hot soup, place a clean towel over the opening.

WHIPPED GARLIC CREAM

1/2 CUP HEAVY (WHIPPING) CREAM

4 MEDIUM GARLIC CLOVES, SLICED

SOUP

2 MEDIUM TO LARGE HEADS GARLIC
   (2 TO 3 OUNCES EACH)

5 CUPS HOMEMADE OR PURCHASED RICH
   CHICKEN BROTH

2 MEDIUM LEEKS (1 INCH IN DIAMETER),
   WHITE AND PALE GREEN PARTS ONLY

1 TABLESPOON UNSALTED BUTTER

2 MEDIUM POTATOES (ABOUT 1 POUND),
   PEELED AND CUT INTO 1/2-INCH
   SLICES

1 CUP HEAVY (WHIPPING) CREAM

3/4 TEASPOON GARLIC POWDER

COARSE SALT, PREFERABLY KOSHER, AND
   WHITE PEPPER

TO MAKE THE WHIPPED CREAM: In a small saucepan over medium heat, combine the cream and garlic. Bring to a simmer and simmer gently for 10 minutes. Remove from the heat, cover, and steep for 20 minutes. Pour the cream through a sieve, discarding the garlic. Cool, cover, and refrigerate the cream until chilled, then whisk or whip to very soft peaks. Makes about 3/4 cup.

TO MAKE THE SOUP: Remove most of the papery outer skin from the garlic heads. Slice off the tops (and discard) to expose the cloves' tips, and transfer to a 2-quart saucepan. Add the chicken broth and bring to a boil over medium-high heat. Reduce the heat to a simmer and cook until the center cloves can be easily pierced with a knife. Remove from the heat and set aside. Using a slotted spoon, remove the garlic and let it cool slightly, reserving the broth. Squeeze the soft cloves out of their skins and set aside.

Cut off the root ends of the leeks and remove the coarse outer leaves. Split lengthwise and separate the leaves under running water to remove any dirt or sand. Cut in 1/8- to 1/4-inch slices.

In a 3-quart saucepan, melt the butter over medium heat and sauté the leeks until soft but not browned, about 8 minutes. Add the potatoes and the reserved broth and garlic, and bring to a boil over medium-high heat. Reduce the heat to a simmer over medium-low to low heat and continue to cook, partially covered, until the potatoes are tender, 25 to 30 minutes.

Remove from the heat and cool slightly. Using a blender, food processor, immersion blender, or food mill, purée the soup, in batches if necessary. Return to the saucepan and stir in the cream. Add the garlic powder and season with salt and pepper to taste. Reheat slowly to serving temperature, stirring often. Do not boil. (The soup can be made 1 day ahead. Cool, then cover and refrigerate. Before serving, bring to a simmer, thinning with broth or milk, if needed.)

To serve, ladle the soup into bowls and garnish with Whipped Garlic Cream. For classic elegance, spoon a dollop of the cream onto the soup and serve. For a more dramatic finish, preheat the broiler, divide the soup among heatproof bowls, dapple the cream across the top, and broil about 4 inches from the heat until flecked with golden brown, 2 to 3 minutes. Serve immediately.

BISTRO VEGETABLE SOUP WITH GARLIC AND BASIL

Serves 4 to 6 (makes about 8 cups)

More like a stew, this robust vegetable soup is a satisfying main course when served with a good, crusty baguette and a salad. Two whole heads of garlic, added at the beginning, give it a wonderful aroma and infusion of flavor. As a bonus, after the garlic has cooked and the cloves are soft and mellow, they are mashed and returned to the soup, giving it extra depth and character. The simple topping, know as *pistou,* adds the zest and fresh taste of raw garlic and basil to the soup. + By the way, this recipe is flexible and leaves plenty of room for touches of your own. If you want to vary or expand the number and kinds of vegetables, go ahead. Add a cup of thinly sliced cabbage, some white beans, even a minced hot pepper or red pepper flakes. For a hint of meat, you can start the soup off by sautéing the leeks and onion in an ounce or two of minced, meaty bacon, or you can round it off by adding some spicy cooked sausage at the end.

SOUP

2 TABLESPOONS EXTRA-VIRGIN OLIVE OIL

1 SMALL LEEK, WHITE PART ONLY, DICED

1 SMALL YELLOW ONION, DICED

1 SMALL CARROT, PEELED AND SLICED INTO
$1/8$ -INCH ROUNDS

1 SMALL CELERY STALK, SLICED

1 MEDIUM (3- TO 4-OUNCE) RED POTATO,
DICED

2 MEDIUM GARLIC HEADS (2 TO $2^{1}/_{2}$ OUNCES
EACH)

1 CAN ($14^{1}/_{2}$ OUNCES) DICED TOMATOES
WITH JUICE

1 TABLESPOON TOMATO PASTE

1 CAN ($15^{1}/_{4}$ OUNCES) PINK PINTO OR
PREMIUM RED BEANS, DRAINED

$1/2$ TEASPOON DRIED THYME

4 CUPS WATER

4 OUNCES FRESH ASPARAGUS, CUT INTO
BITE-SIZE PIECES

1 SMALL ZUCCHINI, CUT LENGTHWISE INTO
QUARTERS AND SLICED

2 TO 3 TABLESPOONS LONG-GRAIN RICE

TO MAKE THE SOUP: In a 6-quart Dutch oven or soup pot, heat the olive oil over medium heat. Add the leek and onion and sauté until soft, 5 minutes. Stir in the carrots, celery, and potato, and sauté for 3 minutes.

Remove most of the papery outer skin from the garlic heads. Using a sharp knife, slice off the tops (and discard) to expose the cloves' tips. Add the garlic heads, tomatoes with juice, tomato paste, beans, thyme, and water. Bring to a boil over medium-high heat, reduce to a simmer, and cook for 20 minutes. Stir in the asparagus, zucchini, and rice, cover partially, and simmer until the rice is done and the garlic cloves are soft, 20 to 30 minutes.

Remove the garlic, and let cool slightly. Squeeze the soft cloves out of their skins and transfer to a small bowl. Add the salt and mash until blended, then stir the mixture back into the soup. Taste and adjust the seasoning, adding pepper to taste.

1 TEASPOON COARSE SALT, PREFERABLY
     KOSHER
FRESHLY GROUND PEPPER

PISTOU
4 LARGE GARLIC CLOVES, PRESSED
     (1$1/2$ TO 2 TEASPOONS)
2 CUPS PACKED FRESH BASIL LEAVES,
     MINCED

FRESHLY GRATED PARMESAN CHEESE
     FOR SERVING

TO MAKE THE *PISTOU*: Before serving, stir or mash together the garlic and basil. Ladle the soup into shallow bowls, top each serving with *pistou,* and serve. At the table, pass the cheese.

CHILLED CUCUMBER SOUP WITH GARLIC AND MINT

Serves 4 to 6 as a first course, 8 to 10 as demitasse appetizer (makes about 4 cups)

This elegant soup has subtle nuances and understated layers of flavor. The cucumbers are sautéed to remove any hint of bitterness, and the garlic and ginger are steeped to bring out their discreet yet zesty character. Present this soup in small servings as an appetizer or first course. In the summer, when we're grilling outdoors, I like to use small African or Asian dipping bowls. For indoor occasions, espresso or demitasse cups do the trick. + Be sure to take the extra measure of straining the soup through a fine sieve. This is the step that gives the soup its sleek and velvety finish.

2 FIRMLY PACKED TABLESPOONS CHOPPED
    GARLIC (ABOUT 3 LARGE CLOVES)
2 TABLESPOONS CHOPPED, UNPEELED
    FRESH GINGER
2 CUPS HALF-AND-HALF
1 TABLESPOON UNSALTED BUTTER
2 LARGE CUCUMBERS, PEELED AND
    SLICED
1 TABLESPOON CHOPPED GREEN ONION,
    BOTH WHITE AND GREEN PARTS
1 LEAFY SPRIG MINT
1/2 TEASPOON COARSE SALT, PREFERABLY
    KOSHER
SNIPPED AND WHOLE FRESH MINT
    LEAVES FOR GARNISHING
CHOPPED PEELED CUCUMBER FOR
    GARNISHING
THINLY SLICED RED RADISH FOR
    GARNISHING (OPTIONAL)

In a medium saucepan, combine the garlic, ginger, and half-and-half over medium-high heat. Bring to a boil, reduce to a gentle simmer, and cook for 10 minutes. Remove from the heat, cover, and steep for 20 minutes. Strain, discarding the garlic and ginger, and set aside.

In a large saucepan, melt the butter over medium-high heat. Add the cucumbers, green onion, and mint sprig and sauté until the cucumbers are soft, 8 to 10 minutes. Add the reserved half-and-half mixture and salt and simmer for 2 to 3 minutes. Remove from the heat and discard the mint sprig. Let cool slightly, then purée in a blender. When puréeing this soup (or any hot liquid) in the blender, be sure the lid is firmly attached, and remove the small plastic insert from the lid. This allows steam to escape. Also, to avoid getting splattered with the hot soup, place a clean towel over the opening.

Strain the soup through a fine sieve, pressing and spreading it with a rubber spatula. Cover and refrigerate until chilled. To serve, garnish with mint, cucumber, and radish, if desired.

SPRING VEGETABLE SOUP WITH TOASTED GARLIC BREAD CRUMBS

Serves 6 to 8 (makes about 9 cups)

Vegetables make a good soup any time of the year, but they are especially welcome in the spring when they're tender and their delicate flavors are bright. One of the culinary treats reserved for the months of March to May is green garlic. It has the look and texture of green onions but the subtle, distinctive flavor of garlic. Teamed with the garlic broth, the green garlic gives this soup its signature appeal. + Orecchiette, the Italian pasta used in this recipe, has a hollowed, oval shape—like little ears—that cradles soups and sauces with every bite. It's a good pasta to stock in your pantry. When it comes to the bread crumbs, either make your own or, if you prefer to purchase them, buy croutons and roughly crush them. Coarse, irregular crumbs will give a delightful texture to the soup.

2 OUNCES DRIED MEDIUM TO SMALL
　　SHELL PASTA, SUCH AS ORECCHIETTE

1 TABLESPOON UNSALTED BUTTER

1 TABLESPOON EXTRA-VIRGIN OLIVE OIL

1 BUNCH (6 TO 8 STALKS) GREEN GARLIC,
　　BOTH BULB AND PALE GREEN PARTS,
　　THINLY SLICED (SEE NOTE)

1 SMALL LEEK, BOTH WHITE AND PALE
　　GREEN PARTS, THINLY SLICED

6 CUPS GARLIC BROTH (PAGE 38)
　　OR VEGETABLE BROTH

12 OUNCES SUGAR SNAP PEAS, CUT
　　DIAGONALLY IN HALF

6 OUNCES FRESH BABY SPINACH
　　(SEE NOTE)

2 TEASPOONS MINCED LEMON ZEST

1 TABLESPOON FRESH LEMON JUICE

COARSE SALT, PREFERABLY KOSHER

1 CUP TOASTED GARLIC BREAD CRUMBS
　　(PAGE 62), FOR SERVING

Using plenty of boiling, salted water, cook the pasta until al dente (tender but firm to the bite), following the package directions. Drain well and set aside.

In a large saucepan over medium-high heat, melt the butter in the olive oil. Add the green garlic and leek and sauté until tender, about 1 minute. Add the broth and bring to a simmer. Add the sugar snap peas and cook over medium heat until just tender, 2 minutes. Stir in the reserved pasta, spinach, lemon zest, and lemon juice. Season to taste with salt. Cook until the spinach is just wilted, about 1 minute. Ladle into warm, shallow soup bowls. At the table, pass the toasted bread crumbs.

NOTE: Reserve some of the flat, slender leaves from the garlic plant, if available, and thinly slice as a garnish. If green garlic is unavailable, substitute another small leek for the recipe but not as a garnish.

To save time, use ready-to-serve, triple-washed, organic young spinach leaves, available in 5- to 7-ounce bags at most supermarkets.

THIS-GETS-MY-VOTE WHITE BEAN SOUP

Serves 6 (makes about 10 cups)

The consensus is in: This homespun soup is a winner wherever it's served. The recipe is based on the famed soup featured in the U.S. Senate's nonpartisan dining rooms, but it's an independent version with the added appeal of roasted garlic. While the beans give the soup its creamy substance, and the ham hock contributes smoky flavor and toothsome bits of meaty ham, it's the golden cloves of garlic that bring out the best in these allies. Make more of this soup than you need. Like a successful incumbent, it is popular from the start and gets even better the second time around.

1 LARGE HEAD ROASTED GARLIC (2 1/2 TO
   3 OUNCES RAW) (SEE PAGE 14)

1 POUND DRIED SMALL WHITE BEANS,
   RINSED AND DRAINED (ABOUT 2 1/2 CUPS)

4 QUARTS COLD WATER, DIVIDED

1 MEATY SMOKED HAM HOCK (10 TO
   12 OUNCES)

1 1/2 TABLESPOONS OLIVE OIL

1 MEDIUM ONION, FINELY CHOPPED

1 1/2 TEASPOONS COARSE SALT,
   PREFERABLY KOSHER

1/2 TEASPOON PEPPER, PREFERABLY
   WHITE

CHOPPED FRESH PARSLEY FOR
   GARNISHING (OPTIONAL)

1 FRENCH BREAD BAGUETTE, CUT IN
   1/3-INCH-THICK SLICES, LIGHTLY
   TOASTED OR GRILLED AND BRUSHED
   WITH OLIVE OIL

When the roasted garlic is cool enough to handle, squeeze the soft cloves from their skins and set aside. In a medium saucepan, combine the beans and 2 quarts of the water. Bring to a brisk boil over high heat and boil for 2 minutes. Remove from the heat, cover, and let stand for 1 hour. Drain, discarding the soaking liquid.

In a 5- to 6-quart soup pot, combine the drained beans, the remaining 2 quarts water, and the ham hock. Bring to a boil over high heat. Reduce the heat to a simmer and cook, covered, until the beans are tender, 2 to 3 hours. (The cooking time will vary depending on the age of the beans.)

Remove the ham hock. When it is cool enough to handle, remove the meat from the bone and dice, discarding the bone, tough outer meat, and excess fat.

Meanwhile, in a medium skillet, heat the olive oil over medium heat and sauté the onion, stirring frequently, until soft but not brown, 8 to 10 minutes. Remove from the heat. Add the reserved garlic to the skillet and, using the back of a spoon, mash the cloves, then stir to combine with the onion.

Return the diced ham and add the roasted garlic mixture to the soup, stir to combine, and season with salt and pepper. Using the back of a spoon, mash some of the beans against the side of the pot to make the soup thick and creamy. Simmer for 30 minutes. (The soup can be made up to 3 days ahead. Cool, cover, and refrigerate, or freeze for up to 3 months.)

To serve, ladle the hot soup into bowls. Sprinkle with parsley, if desired, and serve with toasted French bread.

ROMAINE RIBBONS WITH ROASTED GARLIC DRESSING, BLUE CHEESE, AND TOASTED WALNUTS

Serves 4

This salad is dressed for success and made for entertaining, whether simply tossed with the roasted garlic dressing or embellished with the blue cheese and toasted pecans. Slicing the romaine in flirty, ribbonlike strands adds to the party-perfect allure.

DRESSING

1 LARGE HEAD GARLIC (2^1/$_2$ TO
    3 OUNCES)

2 TABLESPOONS RICE VINEGAR

2 TABLESPOONS APPLE CIDER VINEGAR

2 TO 3 TEASPOONS HONEY, LUKEWARM
    OR AT ROOM TEMPERATURE

1 TEASPOON DIJON MUSTARD

^{1}/$_4$ TEASPOON COARSE SALT, PREFERABLY
    KOSHER

^{1}/$_4$ TEASPOON FRESHLY GROUND PEPPER

5 TABLESPOONS OLIVE OIL

SALAD

1 LARGE HEAD ROMAINE LETTUCE,
    COARSE LEAVES REMOVED, RINSED
    AND PATTED DRY

4 TABLESPOONS (^{1}/$_4$ CUP) CRUMBLED
    BLUE CHEESE, DIVIDED

4 TABLESPOONS (^{1}/$_4$ CUP) COARSELY
    CHOPPED TOASTED WALNUTS OR
    PECANS, DIVIDED (SEE NOTE)

TO MAKE THE DRESSING: Roast the garlic according to the directions on page 14, reserving the oil. Squeeze the soft, golden cloves out of their skins and transfer to a mini-processor. (Leave out any dark, caramelized cloves. They make great nibbles when sprinkled with salt.) Add the rice vinegar, apple cider vinegar, honey, mustard, salt, and pepper and blend until smooth. Add the olive oil and the reserved garlic oil and blend until combined.

TO MAKE THE SALAD: Stack 6 to 8 romaine leaves at a time and cut crosswise into ^{1}/$_2$-inch-wide ribbons. Place the ribbons into a large salad bowl, drizzle with half the dressing, and toss. Taste, adding additional dressing as desired. Divide the salad among 4 salad plates. Garnish each with 1 tablespoon blue cheese and 2 tablespoons walnuts.

NOTE: To toast walnuts or pecans, preheat the oven to 350°F. Spread the nuts on a rimmed baking sheet and bake until lightly browned, about 10 minutes.

ICEBERG WEDGES WITH TIPTOP THOUSAND ISLAND DRESSING

I have nothing against a mesclun salad or a midsummer *caprese* anointed with the designer dressing of the day. But every once in a while, serve me something real and rugged, something with bite and geometry. Give me an iceberg wedge capped with garlicky Thousand Island dressing. Now all that's missing is a thick slab of sirloin steak and a mountain of garlic mashed potatoes.

DRESSING

3 MEDIUM GARLIC CLOVES, MINCED
  (2 1/2 FIRMLY PACKED TEASPOONS)

1/2 CUP MAYONNAISE

1/2 CUP SOUR CREAM

1/4 CUP HEINZ CHILI SAUCE

1 TABLESPOON CHUTNEY SAUCE OR
  PUREED CHUTNEY, SUCH AS MAJOR
  GREY'S

1 TABLESPOON FRESH LEMON JUICE

1/8 TEASPOON CAYENNE PEPPER

1/3 CUP PIMIENTO-STUFFED GREEN
  OLIVES, CHOPPED

PINCH OF FRESHLY GROUND PEPPER, OR
  MORE TO TASTE

1 HEAD ICEBERG LETTUCE, CORED

TO MAKE THE DRESSING: In a medium bowl, mix together the garlic, mayonnaise, sour cream, chili sauce, chutney, lemon juice, and cayenne until blended. Stir in the olives and pepper. Taste and adjust the seasonings. Cover and refrigerate for 3 hours to blend the flavors.

TO PREPARE THE LETTUCE: Cut the lettuce head in half, beginning at the cored end. Cut each half into 2 wedges. Place each wedge on a salad plate, spoon about 3 tablespoons of dressing over each wedge, and serve.

CAESAR SALAD

Serves 4 as a salad course, 2 as an entrée

When it comes to Caesar salads, every garlic lover has strong opinions. Are the leaves left whole to eat with your fingers (as the salad's creator, Caesar Cardini, intended) or torn into pieces to pierce with a fork? Does the dressing include egg? Worcestershire sauce? Anchovy? + The following recipe gives you my answers. If truth be told, I prefer my lettuce torn, but that's just me; the recipe gives alternatives. As for the dressing, there's no need to add Worcestershire sauce. Anchovy paste gives this dressing its characteristic depth and pungency. You'll find several choices when it comes to the egg. Since so many people try to avoid the use of raw eggs in cooking, mayonnaise, coddled egg, and even egg substitute are given as choices. All do the job of coating and glistening the leaves with the garlic-laced dressing, though each gives a slightly different flavor note. It's time to experiment—time to create your own ultimate Caesar.

DRESSING

2 MEDIUM GARLIC CLOVES, HALVED

$1/2$ TEASPOON COARSE SALT, PREFERABLY
KOSHER

1 TEASPOON ANCHOVY PASTE

$1^1/2$ TABLESPOONS MAYONNAISE OR
1 CODDLED EGG (SEE NOTE) OR
2 TABLESPOONS EGG SUBSTITUTE

2 TABLESPOONS FRESH LEMON JUICE

$1/2$ CUP EXTRA-VIRGIN OLIVE OIL

2 TABLESPOONS FRESHLY GRATED
PARMESAN CHEESE

SALAD

2 ROMAINE LETTUCE HEARTS, LEAVES
SEPARATED, OR 1 BAG (10 OUNCES)
ORGANIC HEARTS OF ROMAINE

1 TO $1^1/2$ HEAPING CUPS GARLIC
CROUTONS, HOMEMADE (PAGE 62) OR
PURCHASED

2 TABLESPOONS FRESHLY GRATED
PARMESAN CHEESE

TO MAKE THE DRESSING: Sprinkle the garlic with the salt and mince, pressing the garlic into the salt with the flat of the knife to form a rough paste. Transfer to a small mixing bowl. Whisk in the anchovy paste and mayonnaise. Whisk in the lemon juice. Slowly drizzle in the olive oil with one hand while vigorously whisking the mixture with the other. When the dressing is well combined, whisk in the Parmesan cheese. Taste—it should be slightly salty. Adjust the seasoning and set aside.

TO ASSEMBLE THE SALAD: Leave the romaine leaves whole or tear into bite-sized pieces.

In a large salad bowl, toss the croutons with $1/3$ cup of the dressing. (Coating the croutons first is an important step.) Add the romaine and toss until well coated. Taste, adding additional dressing as desired. Divide the salad among chilled plates, sprinkle with the Parmesan, and serve at once.

NOTE: It is important to use the freshest egg possible, free of cracks and kept refrigerated. Since a raw or coddled egg carries the risk of bacterial growth that can cause salmonella poisoning, it should not be served to people in high-risk groups, such as the elderly, the very young, the chronically ill, and pregnant women.

To coddle an egg, have the egg at room temperature. Place the egg in a small bowl or mug and pour boiling water around the egg until it is covered. Let stand for 1 minute. Immediately run cold water into the bowl until the egg can be easily handled. It can be used immediately.

ASIAN SLAW WITH GARLIC, GINGER, AND CARROT DRESSING

Serves 6

Invest in the Asian market with this flavorful napa cabbage slaw from private chef Suzy Kitman. The asking price is a few simple ingredients, and the tasty dividends are high. The bright, golden-orange dressing has a heady portfolio of high-performance flavors, including fresh garlic and ginger and toasted sesame seed oil. This slaw is the perfect foil for seared tuna, grilled salmon, or barbecued meats. + Unlike its round-headed relatives, napa cabbage (a.k.a. Chinese or celery cabbage) is oblong in shape and has tender, crinkly leaves that are mild and sweet. For a more substantial salad, think about adding small cubes of fresh, firm tofu or sections of mandarin orange.

DRESSING

1 MEDIUM TO LARGE GARLIC CLOVE,
  MINCED (1 TO 1$1/2$ FIRMLY PACKED
  TEASPOONS)

2-INCH PIECE OF SMALL CARROT,
  COARSELY CHOPPED

$1/2$-INCH PIECE OF PEELED GINGER,
  GRATED

$1/4$ CUP RICE WINE VINEGAR

$1/4$ CUP VEGETABLE OIL

1 TABLESPOON ASIAN SESAME OIL

1 TEASPOON COARSE SALT, PREFERABLY
  KOSHER

SLAW

4 CUPS SHREDDED NAPA CABBAGE

3 GREEN ONIONS, BOTH WHITE AND
  GREEN PARTS, CUT DIAGONALLY INTO
  $1/4$-INCH SLICES

2 TABLESPOONS CHOPPED FRESH
  CILANTRO OR PARSLEY

$1/4$ CUP CHOPPED DRY-ROASTED
  CASHEWS OR PEANUTS (OPTIONAL)

TO MAKE THE DRESSING: In a mini-processor or blender, combine the garlic, carrot, ginger, vinegar, vegetable oil, sesame oil, and salt, and blend until puréed.

TO MAKE THE SLAW: In a large bowl, combine the cabbage and green onions. Lightly toss with dressing. Sprinkle with cilantro and cashews, if desired, and serve. (The recipe can be made up to 2 hours ahead. Cover and refrigerate until ready to serve. Longer storage may result in soggy leaves, since napa cabbage is less sturdy than other varieties.)

SUZY'S KIM CHEE

Makes about 2 cups

Personal chef and friend Suzy Kitman loves the hot-sour-salty-sweet garlicky Korean condiment known as kim chee, but she invariably finds the intense chile and garlic flavors in the traditional fermented version too hot for her mouth (or her stomach). Suzy's tasty solution is this fresh, exotic cabbage condiment, which still has plenty of garlicky punch. It's an excellent partner to savory grilled meats or your favorite deli sandwich.

4 CUPS DICED BOK CHOY (1-INCH PIECES)

4 CUPS DICED NAPA CABBAGE (1-INCH PIECES)

3 GREEN ONIONS, BOTH WHITE AND PALE GREEN PARTS, CUT DIAGONALLY INTO $1/8$-INCH SLICES

2 LARGE GARLIC CLOVES, CHOPPED (1 FIRMLY PACKED TABLESPOON PLUS 1 TEASPOON)

$1/2$-INCH PIECE FRESH GINGER, PEELED AND GRATED

$1^1/2$ TEASPOONS CHOPPED JALAPEÑO PEPPER

1 TEASPOON COARSE SALT, PREFERABLY KOSHER

$1/4$ TEASPOON CAYENNE PEPPER OR HOT PAPRIKA, OR MORE TO TASTE

1 TABLESPOON VEGETABLE OIL

1 TABLESPOON PLUS 1 TEASPOON HEINZ CHILI SAUCE

1 LARGE GARLIC CLOVE, PRESSED (OPTIONAL)

In a $2^1/2$- to 3-quart pot, combine the bok choy and cabbage and cover with cold water. Bring to a boil over medium-high heat. Immediately transfer to a colander and rinse with cold water. Drain well, pressing out any excess water (blot with paper towels if desired).

In a medium bowl, toss together the boy choy, cabbage, and green onions. Add the chopped garlic, ginger, jalapeño, salt, and cayenne and toss. Drizzle the oil and chili sauce over the mixture and toss well. Cover and refrigerate for at least 1 hour to let the flavors blend. Taste and adjust the seasoning with cayenne and pressed garlic, if desired.

PANZANELLA

Serves 4 to 6

Although this Tuscan salad was originally used to breathe new life into stale bread, I make it whenever my garden or the farmers' market is bursting with vine-ripened tomatoes. I'll go so far as to buy fresh bread, slice it, and then "stale" it in a low oven (200°F). Some people prefer the crust removed, while others leave it on. I think it's a nice addition that gives texture, color, and crunch to the rustic picnic fare.

6 SLICES DAY-OLD GARLIC OR TUSCAN-
    STYLE BREAD, 1/2 INCH THICK
3 LARGE GARLIC CLOVES, PRESSED
    (ABOUT 1 TABLESPOON)
3 TABLESPOONS RED WINE VINEGAR, OR
    MORE TO TASTE
1 1/2 TEASPOONS FRESH LEMON JUICE
1/2 CUP PLUS 2 TABLESPOONS EXTRA-
    VIRGIN OLIVE OIL
COARSE SALT, PREFERABLY KOSHER, AND
    FRESHLY GROUND PEPPER
4 MEDIUM RIPE TOMATOES (2 POUNDS),
    CORED AND CUT INTO CHUNKS
1/2 MEDIUM RED ONION, CUT IN HALF
    LENGTHWISE AND THINLY SLICED
3/4 CUP LOOSELY PACKED BASIL LEAVES,
    PLUS MORE FOR GARNISHING

Tear the bread into bite-size pieces (you should have 4 to 6 cups) and transfer to a large bowl. Cover the bread with cold water and let soak for 30 minutes.

In a small bowl, whisk together the garlic, vinegar, lemon juice, and olive oil. Season to taste with salt and pepper, and set aside.

In a large salad bowl, combine the tomatoes and onion. Tear the basil into pieces and add to the bowl. Gently squeeze the bread between your palms and add to the bowl. Pour the vinaigrette over the salad and toss. Cover with plastic wrap and let rest, at room temperature or refrigerated, for 30 minutes or up to 3 hours. Before serving, taste and adjust the seasoning with vinegar if necessary. Garnish with additional basil leaves and serve.

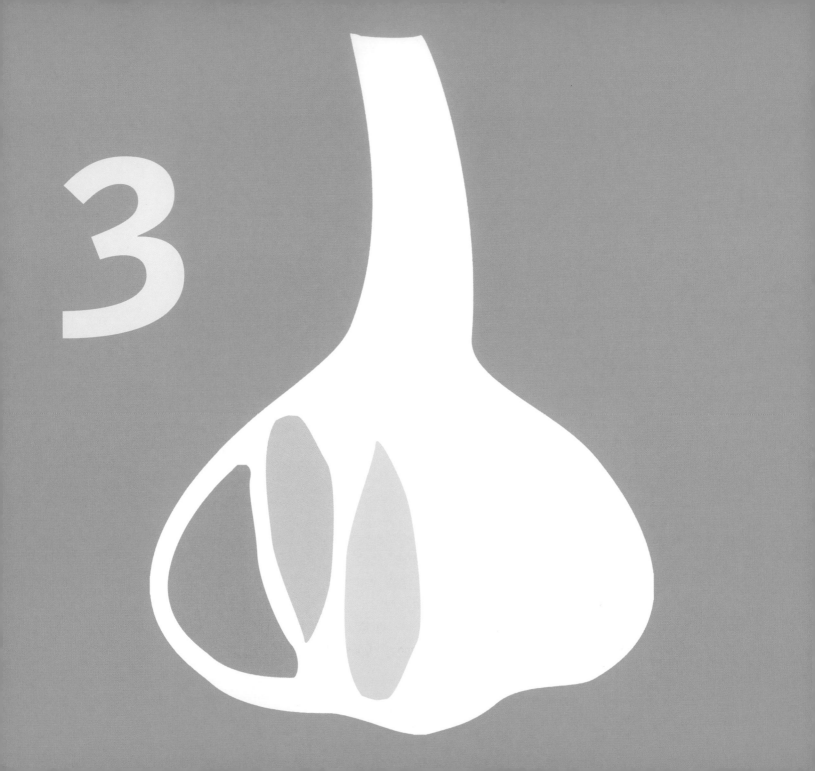

BREADS, PIZZAS, AND TASTY SANDWICHES

Any way you slice it—it's gotta have garlic

HIS GARLIC BREAD/MY GARLIC BREAD—YOU DECIDE!

Serves 4 to 6

My dad was a rocket scientist, a great horseman, and the guy in charge of garlic bread on family spaghetti nights. A man of the '50s, with brains and agility, he mixed margarine with Lawry's garlic salt and slathered it between the spongy slices of supermarket French bread. Then he sprinkled it with paprika, wrapped it tightly in foil, and baked it. We loved every salty, soggy slice. Still do. + I'm a cook and a writer; I ride bareback with the best of them; and when it's my family's spaghetti night, I still make my dad's garlic bread, as well as my own. I use rustic Italian bread. I make the garlic butter with fresh garlic, tender parsley, real butter, and extra-virgin olive oil, and I don't overdo it on the spreading. Funny thing—both versions of this old favorite disappear. It's up to you to decide which one you'll fix—or you too may decide to serve both. + You'll notice that both are baked in foil. That's the way my dad did it, and I think it makes for a softer, tastier interior. (The foil keeps things a bit cleaner, too.) Many people prefer to "steam" the bread in a wet paper bag. Also, it's a good idea to briefly sauté the garlic. This gets rid of any possible bitterness while still retaining that great garlic flavor.

MY GARLIC BREAD

3 MEDIUM GARLIC CLOVES, CUT IN HALF

3/4 TEASPOON COARSE SALT, PREFERABLY KOSHER

3 TABLESPOONS EXTRA-VIRGIN OLIVE OIL

3 TABLESPOONS UNSALTED BUTTER

1 TABLESPOON MINCED FRESH PARSLEY

1 LOAF (15 BY 3 1/2 INCHES) PEASANT OR RUSTIC ITALIAN BREAD

HIS GARLIC BREAD

6 TABLESPOONS MARGARINE, AT ROOM TEMPERATURE

1 1/2 TEASPOONS GARLIC SALT OR GARLIC PARSLEY SALT

1 LOAF SUPERMARKET ITALIAN BREAD

PAPRIKA FOR DUSTING

Preheat the oven to 350°F.

FOR MY GARLIC BREAD: Sprinkle the garlic with the salt and mince, pressing the garlic into the salt with the flat of the knife to form a rough paste. Transfer to a small sauté pan, add the olive oil, and sauté over medium-low heat, stirring, for 5 minutes. Do not let brown.

In a small bowl, combine the butter with the hot garlic oil mixture. Add the parsley and stir until combined and spreadable.

Using a serrated knife, make diagonal slices in the bread at 3/4- to 1-inch intervals without cutting all the way through, stopping short of the bottom crust. "Sensibly" brush or spread the garlic butter into each cut. Wrap the loaf in foil.

FOR HIS GARLIC BREAD: In a small bowl, mix together the margarine and garlic salt until blended and spreadable.

Using a serrated knife, make diagonal slices in the bread at 3/4- to 1-inch intervals without cutting all the way through, stopping short of the bottom crust. Liberally brush or spread the garlic butter into each cut, then dust with paprika. Wrap the loaf in foil.

Bake the loaves for 15 minutes. Open the foil on both loaves and bake until the crusts are crisp, 10 to 15 minutes.

For **ONE-AND-ONLY GARLIC BREAD SLICES,** preheat the broiler. Spread one side of individual slices with either garlic butter topping. Arrange on a baking sheet and broil, watching carefully, until the topping begins to bubble and the bread just begins to brown.

For **GARLIC BREAD BATONS,** preheat the broiler. Using a serrated knife, slice off both ends from 2 French bread baguettes (22 by 3 inches). Split each loaf in half lengthwise. Then cut each piece in half crosswise. You will have 8 slices. Cut each slice lengthwise into thirds and arrange them on a baking sheet. Lightly spread the cut sides with either garlic butter topping. Broil, watching carefully, until the batons just begin to brown.

GARLIC CROUTONS FOR ONE AND ALL

What's the difference between a good salad and a great salad? The croutons, of course. (That goes for good and great soups, too.) Here are three classic versions for your tasting pleasure. Plus, if dinner is in the oven and the croutons are missing, I've included a last-minute quickie method. + All the recipes use a fine-grained loaf of Italian bread made with semolina flour. You can substitute another fine-grained bread if you wish; just avoid bread with large air pockets. + For tasty **TOASTED GARLIC BREAD CRUMBS,** you can't go wrong if you start with any one of these recipes. When making the crumbs, keep them irregular and coarse, about the size of dried black beans, so they give texture and bite to your food (unless you're using them as a filler for meatloaf). When bread crumbs are too fine, they're too close to sawdust. For rough crumbs, put the croutons in a plastic bag and use a rolling pin to crush them. For fine crumbs, use a food processor.

GARLIC CROUTONS

Makes 8 cups

1/3 CUP PLUS 1 TABLESPOON EXTRA-
   VIRGIN OLIVE OIL
4 MEDIUM GARLIC CLOVES, MINCED
   (1 FIRMLY PACKED TABLESPOON)
1/2 TEASPOON COARSE SALT, PREFERABLY
   KOSHER
8 CUPS SLIGHTLY STALE 1/2-INCH BREAD
   CUBES, CUT FROM A FINE-GRAINED
   ITALIAN SEMOLINA BREAD
   (11/4 POUNDS) (SEE HEADNOTE ON
   PAGE 57)
PINCH OF SUGAR

Preheat the oven to 300°F.

In a small bowl, mix together the olive oil, garlic, and salt. In a large bowl, drizzle the olive oil mixture over the bread cubes and toss until evenly coated. Sprinkle with the sugar and toss again.

On 2 rimmed baking sheets, spread the croutons in a single layer and bake, stirring occasionally, until golden and crisp, about 25 minutes. Turn the croutons midway to guarantee even browning. When cool, store in an airtight container.

PARMESAN GARLIC CROUTONS

Makes 8 cups

3 TABLESPOONS UNSALTED BUTTER,
   MELTED
3 TABLESPOONS EXTRA-VIRGIN OLIVE OIL
4 MEDIUM GARLIC CLOVES, MINCED
   (1 FIRMLY PACKED TABLESPOON)
$1/2$ TEASPOON COARSE SALT, PREFERABLY
   KOSHER
8 CUPS SLIGHTLY STALE $1/2$-INCH BREAD
   CUBES, CUT FROM A FINE-GRAINED
   ITALIAN SEMOLINA BREAD
   ($1 1/4$ POUNDS) (SEE HEADNOTE ON
   PAGE 57)
$1/4$ CUP FRESHLY GRATED PARMESAN
   CHEESE
PINCH OF SUGAR

Preheat the oven to 300°F.

In a small bowl, mix together the butter, olive oil, garlic, and salt. In a large bowl, drizzle the olive oil mixture over the bread cubes and toss until evenly coated. Sprinkle the cheese and sugar over the bread cubes and toss until all the cheese is covering the bread cubes.

On 2 rimmed baking sheets, spread the croutons in a single layer and bake, stirring occasionally, until golden and crisp, about 25 minutes. Turn the croutons midway to guarantee even browning. When cool, store in an airtight container.

HERB GARLIC CROUTONS

Makes 8 cups

3 TABLESPOONS UNSALTED BUTTER,
   MELTED

3 TABLESPOONS EXTRA-VIRGIN OLIVE OIL

4 MEDIUM GARLIC CLOVES, MINCED
   (1 FIRMLY PACKED TABLESPOON)

1/2 TEASPOON DRIED RED PEPPER FLAKES

1/2 TEASPOON MINCED FRESH OREGANO

2 TEASPOONS MINCED FRESH PARSLEY

1/4 TO 1/2 TEASPOON MINCED FRESH
   ROSEMARY

1/2 TEASPOON COARSE SALT, PREFERABLY
   KOSHER

8 CUPS SLIGHTLY STALE 1/2-INCH BREAD
   CUBES, CUT FROM A FINE-GRAINED
   ITALIAN SEMOLINA BREAD
   (11/4 POUNDS) (SEE HEADNOTE ON
   PAGE 57)

PINCH OF SUGAR

Preheat the oven to 300°F.

In a small bowl, mix together the butter, olive oil, garlic, red pepper flakes, oregano, parsley, rosemary, and salt. In a large bowl, drizzle the olive oil mixture over the bread cubes and toss until evenly coated. Sprinkle with the sugar and toss again.

On 2 rimmed baking sheets, spread the croutons in a single layer and bake, stirring occasionally, until golden and crisp, about 25 minutes. Turn the croutons midway to guarantee even browning. When cool, store in an airtight container.

OUT OF CROUTONS? TIME FOR DINNER? CROUTONS

Preheat the oven to 300°F. Brush both sides of three 1/2-inch-thick slices of fine-grained white, Italian, or French bread with olive oil and sprinkle with garlic salt. Cut the bread into 1/2-inch cubes, place on a rimmed baking sheet, and bake until crisp, 20 to 25 minutes. Sprinkle with grated Parmesan cheese and cool.

GARLIC FOCACCIA

Makes twelve 3-inch squares

Foccacia is really just a thick pizza. Unlike its slender relative, foccacia usually has fewer toppings and is served as a bread alongside other entrées. This traditional recipe, with thin slivers of garlic lightly flavoring the olive oil, partners perfectly with anything you might offer.

TOPPING

1/4 CUP EXTRA-VIRGIN OLIVE OIL

8 TO 10 MEDIUM GARLIC CLOVES, VERY
    THINLY SLICED

DOUGH

1 CUP WARM WATER (105°F TO 115°F)

1 TEASPOON SUGAR

1 PACKAGE (1 TABLESPOON) ACTIVE DRY
    YEAST

2 3/4 CUPS ALL-PURPOSE FLOUR

1/4 CUP SEMOLINA FLOUR

1/4 CUP FINELY GROUND YELLOW CORNMEAL

1 TEASPOON COARSE SALT, PREFERABLY
    KOSHER

1 TEASPOON COARSE SALT, PREFERABLY
    KOSHER

TO MAKE THE TOPPING: In a small bowl, combine the oil and garlic and set aside.

TO MAKE THE DOUGH: In a small bowl, mix together the water and sugar. Sprinkle the yeast over the water and stir gently. Let stand until the surface has a thick layer of foam, about 5 minutes.

In the bowl of a heavy-duty mixer, combine the all-purpose flour, semolina, cornmeal, and salt. Using the paddle attachment, mix on low speed to blend for 1 minute. Add the yeast mixture and mix on medium speed for 1 minute.

Change to the dough hook and knead on medium speed until the dough is smooth, resilient, and elastic, about 5 minutes. Shape the dough into a ball and put it in a large, oiled bowl, turning the dough so that the surface is covered with oil. Cover tightly with plastic wrap and let the dough rise in a warm, draft-free place until it has doubled in size, 1 1/2 to 2 hours.

Lightly oil a 13-by-9-inch baking pan. Using lightly oiled hands, press the dough out to cover the bottom of the pan. (If the dough is too sticky and resistant, cover it with a towel and let it rest for 10 minutes; then stretch again.) Cover with a towel and let rise until the dough is full of air bubbles, 45 minutes to 1 hour.

Preheat the oven to 425°F. Arrange an oven rack in the lower third of the oven.

Using your fingers, dimple the dough. Drizzle the topping over the dough and, with clean fingers or a brush, make sure it settles in the indentations and covers the top, including the edges. Evenly distribute the garlic slices. Sprinkle the topping with the salt. Bake until the foccacia is golden brown, 20 to 25 minutes.

PIZZA BIANCO WITH ROASTED GARLIC AND FINGERLING POTATOES

Serves 4

Nowadays you can top a pizza with just about anything. When I want to relish the mellow, slightly sweet taste of roasted garlic, I'll fix a *pizza bianco*. It's easy to do, especially with frozen pizza dough on hand. Instead of a tomato sauce base, I'll spread a layer of soft, mild ricotta, and then arrange wedges of fingerling potatoes over the top. Next come the golden cloves, as many as I can handle, and, for an accent, fresh sage and capers. My, oh my, it's not only pretty to look at, it's full of beautiful and delicious secrets!

2 MEDIUM HEADS ROASTED GARLIC (2 TO
   2 1/2 OUNCES EACH RAW) (SEE PAGE 14)

8 OUNCES FROZEN PIZZA OR BREAD
   DOUGH, THAWED

1/4 CUP EXTRA-VIRGIN OLIVE OIL

3 MEDIUM GARLIC CLOVES, PRESSED
   (ABOUT 1 TABLESPOON)

6 OUNCES FINGERLING POTATOES,
   PARBOILED

1 CONTAINER (15 OUNCES) WHOLE-MILK
   RICOTTA CHEESE

1 TABLESPOON FRESH SAGE LEAVES,
   COARSELY CHOPPED

16 TO 20 CAPERS, DRAINED AND RINSED

COARSE SALT, PREFERABLY KOSHER

Preheat the oven to 425°F.

When the roasted garlic is cool enough to handle, squeeze the soft cloves from their skins and set aside. Dust 2 baking sheets with cornmeal and set aside. Place the dough on a lightly floured surface and divide into 4 pieces. Roll out each piece to a 4-inch round. Set aside for 10 minutes. Then roll out each piece to an 8-inch, 1/8-inch-thick round. Arrange 2 dough rounds on each baking sheet. Roll the edges of each round over to create a thin lip. Refrigerate until chilled, about 30 minutes.

Arrange the oven racks in the lower third of the oven.

In a small bowl, combine the olive oil and pressed garlic, and set aside. Cut the potatoes in quarters or eighths lengthwise, and set aside. (You should have 6 to 8 pieces per pizza.)

Remove the crusts from the refrigerator and brush the tops as well as the edges with the garlic olive oil. Using the back of a spoon or clean fingers, spread about 1/2 cup of ricotta over each pizza, leaving the lip plain. Arrange the potatoes in a circular pattern radiating from the center. Divide and sprinkle the garlic cloves, sage, and 4 or 5 capers around the potatoes on each pizza. Drizzle with the remaining garlic olive oil and sprinkle liberally with salt.

Bake until the potatoes and the crusts are brown, 10 to 12 minutes.

CONEY ISLAND HOT DOGS WITH DAMN-GOOD GARLIC SAUCE

Serves 4 to 6

While a Coney Island vendor named Charles Feltman may be credited with introducing the "hot dog" in a bun in the 1890s, it was in 1914 that a Michigan man, George Todoroff, introduced the chili topping to go along with the mustard and onions. Over the next three decades, his Great Lakes restaurant sold more than 17 million Coney Island hot dogs. No doubt this damn-good garlic sauce would have doubled that number.

SAUCE

1 SMALL YELLOW ONION, FINELY CHOPPED

2 TABLESPOONS OLIVE OIL

$^2/_3$ CUP FIRMLY PACKED CHOPPED GARLIC
   (ABOUT 1$^1/_2$ LARGE GARLIC HEADS)

1 CAN (14$^1/_2$ OUNCES) CRUSHED TOMATOES

1 CAN (8 OUNCES) TOMATO SAUCE

1 CUP WATER

1$^1/_2$ TABLESPOONS CHILI POWDER

1 SCANT TABLESPOON PACKED BROWN
   SUGAR

1 TEASPOON GROUND CUMIN

1 TEASPOON PAPRIKA

$^1/_2$ TEASPOON COARSE SALT, PREFERABLY
   KOSHER, OR MORE TO TASTE

12 OUNCES GROUND CHUCK, COOKED AND
   CRUMBLED

HOT DOGS

4 TO 6 LARGE SOFT, WHITE HOT DOG BUNS,
   SPLIT BUT NOT SEPARATED

4 TABLESPOONS ($^1/_2$ STICK) UNSALTED
   BUTTER, AT ROOM TEMPERATURE

4 TO 6 LARGE HOT DOGS, GRILLED OR
   COOKED AS DESIRED

1 SMALL SWEET ONION, FINELY CHOPPED

TANGY YELLOW MUSTARD FOR SERVING

TO MAKE THE SAUCE: In a small skillet, sauté the onion in the olive oil over medium-low heat, stirring frequently, until translucent. Add the garlic and stir constantly until fragrant, 1 to 2 minutes. Do not let brown.

In a large saucepan over medium heat, combine the tomatoes, tomato sauce, water, garlic mixture, chili powder, brown sugar, cumin, paprika, and salt. Bring to a boil and reduce the heat to a simmer over medium-low to low heat. Continue to cook, stirring occasionally, until thick, about 1$^1/_2$ hours. Stir in the crumbled meat. Taste and adjust the seasoning with salt and chili powder.

TO ASSEMBLE THE HOT DOGS: Heat a large skillet over medium heat. Butter the buns, add them to the skillet, buttered side down, and toast until golden, about 1 minute. (You also can steam the buns, as George Todoroff did with the originals.)

Place the split buns on individual plates. Lay a hog dog on each bun. Spoon sauce over each hot dog and garnish with onion and mustard. Serve with a big napkin to satisfy a big appetite. (By the way, neatness doesn't matter.)

VARIATION:

As long as we're drawing on marvelous, messy mealtime memories, here's a recipe for a **DAMN-GOOD SLOPPY JOE.** Cook the sauce as described in the recipe, using 1$^1/_2$ pounds ground chuck. Simmer the mixture, stirring occasionally, until thick enough to spread on a sandwich. To serve, split and toast a soft, white hamburger bun. Ladle $^1/_2$ to $^2/_3$ cup of the sauce onto the bottom half of the bun, add the bun top, and serve immediately.

AÏOLI TUNA MELT

Serves 2

Remember the tuna sandwich your mom used to make for your lunchbox?
Forgettaboutit.
Miracle Whip? Out the door.
Sliced yellow cheese? For the kids.

Here's a tuna melt for wowing grown-up friends and hearty appetites. With its garlicky homemade aïoli and the mild and nutty fontina cheese, it's vividly and immediately satisfying. Choose the open-faced English muffin version for knife and fork occasions, or go for the gusto with the variation that follows. Made with easy-to-hold bread and crispy bacon, this scrumptious fried sandwich will make your day. + Okay, nobody's looking—if you're in a hurry, doctor your favorite purchased mayonnaise with the garlic and capers. Sometimes a craving needs to be satisfied.

1 CAN (6 OUNCES) WATER- OR OIL-PACKED
   TUNA, WELL DRAINED

1 MEDIUM GARLIC CLOVE, PRESSED
   (1/2 TEASPOON)

1 TEASPOON CAPERS, DRAINED, RINSED,
   AND COARSELY CHOPPED

4 TO 6 TABLESPOONS AÏOLI (PAGE 27),
   DIVIDED

COARSE SALT, PREFERABLY KOSHER, AND
   FRESHLY GROUND PEPPER

2 SPLIT AND PARTIALLY TOASTED
   ENGLISH MUFFINS

4 OUNCES FONTINA CHEESE, GRATED
   (ABOUT 1 CUP)

Preheat the broiler.

In a small bowl, flake the tuna. Add the garlic and capers and mix until blended. Add 4 tablespoons of aïoli and mix until combined. Season to taste with the salt and pepper, adding the remaining 2 tablespoons of aïoli to taste.

Divide the tuna mixture among the 4 muffin slices. Place the muffins on a broiler pan. Divide and sprinkle the grated cheese over the tuna. Broil until the cheese melts and begins to bubble, 2 to 4 minutes. Watch carefully; browning time will vary depending on the thickness of the sandwich and its distance from the broiler.

VARIATION:

For the ultimate **AÏOLI BACON TUNA MELT,** substitute 4 slices good-quality white bread for the split English muffins. Arrange the bread slices in pairs, and sprinkle some of the cheese on each slice. Next, arrange 1 or 2 slices of your favorite crisply cooked smoked bacon on 2 of the slices and cover with the tuna mixture. Gently invert the opposite bread slices and press together. In a skillet over medium heat, melt 1 tablespoon butter. Add the sandwiches and cook until lightly toasted on the bottom. Flip, adding more butter if necessary, and cook until the cheese has melted and the bread is lightly toasted. Enjoy!

GRILLED GARLIC BRUSCHETTA WITH BASIL, TOMATO, AND FRESH MOZZARELLA

Serves 4

In the summer, this is my idea of an easy meal. I've also cut the slices into small pieces to enjoy as appetizers while barbecuing the main course. + For even more of a garlic fest, as a variation, dot the bruschetta with sweet cloves of roasted garlic just before serving. + By the way, *bruschetta* comes from the Italian word *bruciare,* meaning "to toast or to burn." Let's go for the former. (It's not hard to pronounce. Just put a *k* in the middle.)

1 FRENCH BREAD BAGUETTE (ABOUT 15 OUNCES)

4 LARGE GARLIC CLOVES, CUT IN HALF

1/2 TEASPOON COARSE SALT, PREFERABLY KOSHER

2 TABLESPOONS UNSALTED BUTTER, AT ROOM TEMPERATURE

1 TABLESPOON OLIVE OIL

2 TABLESPOONS MINCED FRESH FLAT-LEAF PARSLEY

2 TABLESPOONS MINCED FRESH BASIL LEAVES

2 BALLS (4 TO 5 OUNCES EACH) FRESH MOZZARELLA CHEESE, SLICED

4 SMALL VINE-RIPENED TOMATOES, AT ROOM TEMPERATURE, SLICED IN 4 ROUNDS EACH

2 TO 4 TABLESPOONS GRATED PARMESAN CHEESE (OPTIONAL)

8 TO 16 TINY BASIL LEAVES FOR GARNISHING

Light a medium to medium-low fire in a gas or charcoal grill.

Cut the baguette in half crosswise. Cut each piece in half lengthwise to form 4 pieces. Sprinkle the garlic with the salt and mince, pressing the garlic into the salt with the flat of the knife to form a rough paste. Transfer to a small bowl, add the butter, oil, parsley, and basil, and stir until blended. Spread the garlic butter mixture on all cut sides of the bread.

Just before grilling the bread, wipe the grill rack from back to front with a clean rag dipped in vegetable oil. (If you go from front to back, you might lose some hair on your arm.)

Grill the bread, cut sides down, until lightly toasted, 1 to 2 minutes. Remove from the grill. Quickly arrange the mozzarella on the cut sides of the toast, dividing it evenly. Return the open-face sandwiches to the grill, cut side up. Cook until the bottom sides are toasted and the cheese warms and softens, about 2 minutes. (You'll have to make sure the coals are at medium-low heat so the bread won't get too brown.) Remove from the grill and top with the tomatoes, dividing them evenly. Sprinkle with Parmesan cheese, if desired, and garnish every, or every other, tomato round with a tiny basil leaf. Cut each sandwich diagonally in half, and serve at once.

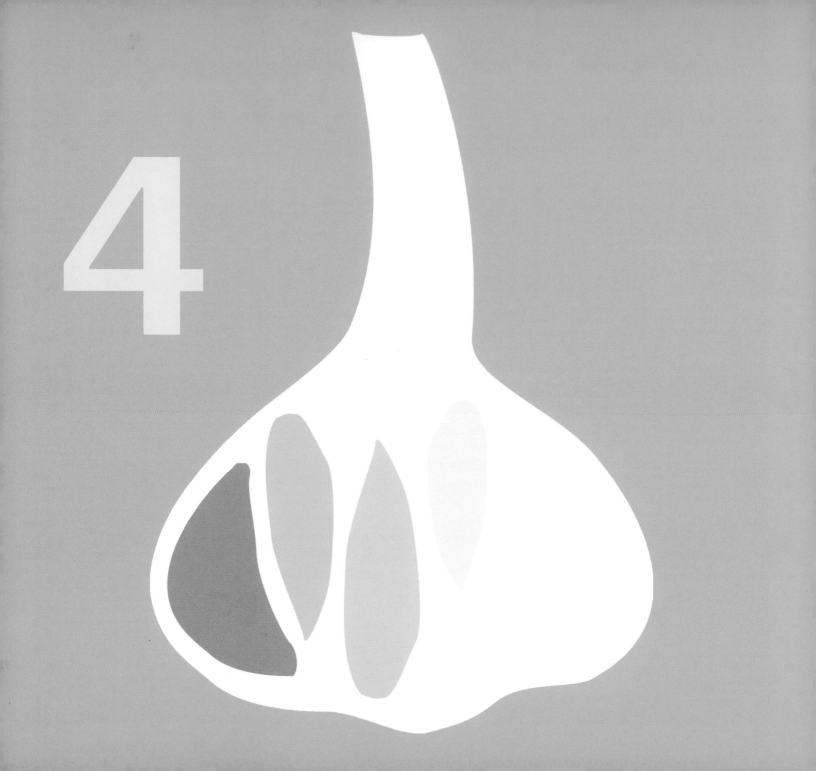

PASTAS AND RISOTTOS
Garlic galore—the Italians got it right!

SPAGHETTI AGLIO E OLIO

Serves 2

Garlic, olive oil, and spaghetti—three indispensable ingredients that add up to one classic Italian pasta dish. It's quick to prepare, delicious to eat, and inexpensive too. But remember, you get what you pay for. So be sure to use the freshest and best ingredients you can find: plump, firm garlic; extra-virgin olive oil; and pasta made from semolina flour. The parsley, which accents the dish with color and flavor, also deserves consideration. Although this recipe calls for the fresh, flat-leaf Italian variety, if you find its leaves are tough or bitter (go ahead, take a nibble), look for a tender, curly-leaf parsley.

8 OUNCES DRIED SPAGHETTI, LINGUINE, OR CAPELLINI

1/2 CUP EXTRA-VIRGIN OLIVE OIL

4 LARGE GARLIC CLOVES, MINCED (2 FIRMLY PACKED TABLESPOONS)

1/4 TO 1/2 TEASPOON DRIED RED PEPPER FLAKES

1/3 CUP FINELY CHOPPED, TENDER FLAT-LEAF PARSLEY LEAVES, LOOSELY PACKED

GRATED PECORINO ROMANO CHEESE FOR SERVING

COARSE SALT, PREFERABLY KOSHER, AND FRESHLY GROUND PEPPER

Prepare the spaghetti according to the package directions. Using plenty of boiling salted water, cook the spaghetti until al dente (tender but firm to the bite), reserving 1/2 cup of the pasta water. (Serving hint: As the pasta water heats, place your serving bowl or platter over the pot to warm it.) Drain and transfer to a warm serving bowl or platter.

Meanwhile, in a small saucepan, heat the olive oil over medium-low heat, add the garlic and the red pepper flakes, and sauté until the garlic is fragrant and just begins to color but not brown, about 5 minutes. Remove from the heat, drizzle over the pasta, and toss. Add the parsley and lightly toss again. If the mixture seems too dry, toss in a little of the reserved pasta water. Serve at once in warm, shallow bowls. At the table, pass the cheese and season with salt and pepper to taste.

VARIATIONS:

Hungry for something extra? **"LET'S ADD MORE" GARLIC PASTA** gives you the option of adding one or more of the following when tossing in the parsley:

1 TABLESPOON OR MORE GRATED LEMON ZEST

3 TABLESPOONS OR MORE CHOPPED FRESH OR TOASTED WALNUTS

3 TABLESPOONS OR MORE SMALL CAPERS

2 TO 3 TABLESPOONS CRUSHED GARLIC CROUTONS (PAGE 62)

1 CAN (6 OUNCES) OLIVE-OIL-PACKED TUNA, DRAINED AND FLAKED

SLICED MUSHROOMS OR OTHER FAVORITE VEGETABLES, BRIEFLY SAUTÉED IN OLIVE OIL OR
    ADDED TO THE PASTA WATER FOR THE LAST MINUTE OF COOKING

For **PENNE ALL'ARRABBIATA,** follow the master recipe, using penne for the pasta, and then proceed as directed. Substitute a medium saucepan for the small one to sauté the garlic until it begins to color. Then stir in 1 can (28 ounces) crushed Italian plum tomatoes. (Or place a food mill over the saucepan and purée one 28-ounce can of whole Italian plum tomatoes with their juices directly into the saucepan.) Simmer, stirring occasionally, until the sauce is slightly reduced, about 25 minutes. Taste, adjust the seasoning with salt, and proceed as directed.

PASTA WITH ROASTED TOMATO, GARLIC, AND FRESH MOZZARELLA

Serves 4

The enticing aroma of tomatoes and garlic roasting in the oven is reason enough to make this dish. But after one taste, you'll discover why this simple recipe is a family favorite that's great for entertaining too. The art is all in the presentation: Spoon some of the rich sauce down the middle of the pasta, leaving plain pasta on either side. Then top the plain pasta with cubes of fresh mozzarella, which warm and soften right away. Now enjoy one intense, sauce-drenched bite, followed by one creamy bite. Skipping between the two pleasures yields double delight.

3 TABLESPOONS EXTRA-VIRGIN OLIVE OIL

6 TO 7 LARGE GARLIC CLOVES, MINCED
(ABOUT 3 TABLESPOONS)

1/4 TEASPOON DRIED RED PEPPER FLAKES

6 TO 8 MEDIUM RIPE TOMATOES
(3 POUNDS), CORED AND CUT INTO
EIGHTHS

1/2 CUP CHOPPED FRESH BASIL LEAVES

1/2 TEASPOON COARSE SALT, PREFERABLY
KOSHER

1 TABLESPOON SMALL CAPERS

1 1/2 TEASPOONS ANCHOVY PASTE

1 POUND FARFALLE (BOW-TIE) OR
FUSILLI (CORKSCREW) PASTA

1 BALL FRESH MOZZARELLA CHEESE
(ABOUT 4 OUNCES), CUT INTO 1/2-INCH
CUBES

1 CUP FRESHLY GRATED PARMIGIANO-
REGGIANO CHEESE

COARSE SALT, PREFERABLY KOSHER, AND
FRESHLY GROUND PEPPER

Preheat the oven to 375°F.

In a 13-by-9-by-2-inch glass baking dish, combine the olive oil, garlic, and red pepper flakes. Add the tomatoes and gently toss. Roast, stirring occasionally, for 45 minutes. Stir in the basil and the 1/2 teaspoon salt and continue to roast for 15 minutes. Stir in the capers and the anchovy paste and continue to roast until the tomatoes darken and the juices concentrate, 25 to 40 minutes. (The time will vary depending on the juiciness of the tomatoes.) Set aside. (The sauce can be made up to 2 hours ahead and left to stand at room temperature. Or cool, cover, and refrigerate for up to 3 days; freeze for up to 3 months. To serve, reheat over medium-low heat.)

Meanwhile, prepare the pasta according to the package directions. Using plenty of boiling salted water, cook the pasta until al dente (tender but firm to the bite). Drain well and divide the pasta among warm, shallow bowls.

To serve, spoon about 1/3 cup of the sauce along the center of each serving. Arrange the mozzarella cubes along either side of the sauce on the plain pasta. Sprinkle each serving with a dusting of Parmigiano-Reggiano. At the table, season with additional Parmigiano-Reggiano and salt and pepper to taste.

SPAGHETTI WITH MOM'S THICK AND MEATY MARINARA SAUCE

Serves **8**

Nothing could be finer than my mom's spaghetti and meat sauce, my dad's foil-wrapped garlic bread (page 60), a mixed green salad dressed with a lemony garlic vinaigrette, and some scoops of Neapolitan ice cream corralled on a TV tray just in time to catch *Gunsmoke*. Good stuff, really (who can argue with the aromas, flavors, and heroes of childhood?). So when you look at this recipe and discover all forms of tomato from a can as well as garlic from a jar, don't be sideswiped. This is one dynamite sauce. It's simple. It's substantial. It gets better with age.

12 OUNCES LEAN GROUND BEEF

12 OUNCES MILD ITALIAN SAUSAGE

2 TABLESPOONS OLIVE OIL

1 LARGE YELLOW ONION, FINELY CHOPPED
(ABOUT 1²/₃ CUPS)

8 LARGE GARLIC CLOVES, FINELY CHOPPED
(ABOUT ¹/₄ CUP)

3 CELERY STALKS, DICED

2 MEDIUM CARROTS, PEELED AND GRATED

³/₄ CUP RED TABLE WINE

1 CAN (11¹/₂ OUNCES) TOMATO JUICE

1 CAN (15 OUNCES) TOMATO SAUCE

1 CAN (6 OUNCES) TOMATO PASTE

1 CUP WATER

¹/₂ TEASPOON DRIED RED PEPPER FLAKES

2 TABLESPOONS GARLIC POWDER

¹/₂ TEASPOON PAPRIKA

¹/₂ TEASPOON CHILI POWDER

1 TABLESPOON DRIED OREGANO

1 TABLESPOON DRIED BASIL

1¹/₂ TEASPOONS DRIED THYME

GARLIC SALT AND FRESHLY GROUND
PEPPER (OPTIONAL)

2 POUNDS DRIED SPAGHETTI

¹/₂ CUP MINCED FRESH PARSLEY FOR
GARNISHING (OPTIONAL)

In a large skillet, sauté the beef and the sausage over medium heat until just brown, using a wooden spoon or a knife and fork to finely crumble the meat.

Meanwhile, in a large Dutch oven, heat the olive oil over medium heat and sauté the onion until translucent. Add the garlic, celery, and carrots and continue to sauté, stirring constantly, until all the vegetables are soft, about 7 minutes.

Stir in the wine, tomato juice, tomato sauce, tomato paste, and water. Stir in the red pepper flakes, garlic powder, paprika, chili powder, oregano, basil, and thyme. With a slotted spoon, transfer the beef and sausage to the Dutch oven and stir until blended. The sauce will be thick. Bring to a simmer, cover, and cook, stirring occasionally, for about 45 minutes. Taste and adjust the seasoning with garlic salt and pepper, if desired. (Often this sauce does not need extra salt or pepper.) Turn the heat off, cover, and set aside to let the flavors blend, 1 to 2 hours. To serve, reheat the sauce until heated through. (The sauce can be made up to 3 days ahead. Cool, cover, and refrigerate, or freeze for up to 3 months.) Makes about 10 cups.

Prepare the spaghetti according to the package directions. Using plenty of boiling salted water, cook the spaghetti until al dente (tender but firm to the bite). Drain well and divide the pasta among 8 plates.

To serve, ladle a healthy amount of thick sauce down the center of each serving, reserving any extra for the freezer (and a quick meal). Garnish with parsley, if desired, and serve.

SIX CLOVES MAC AND CHEESE

Serves 4

I always thought my garlicky macaroni and cheese was rich, creamy, and right on the mark, but then I sampled Oregon chef Leather Storr's macaroni and cheese accented with bay and allspice. This combination of aromatic herb and savory-sweet spice was enough to make me revise my tried-and-true recipe, with great-tasting results. See what you think.

2 CUPS WHOLE MILK

1 CAN (14 OUNCES) EVAPORATED MILK

6 LARGE GARLIC CLOVES, MINCED
   (ABOUT 2 PACKED TABLESPOONS)

1 LARGE BAY LEAF

4 WHOLE ALLSPICE BERRIES

1/4 TEASPOON DRIED RED PEPPER FLAKES

1 TEASPOON COARSE SALT, PREFERABLY
   KOSHER

4 1/2 TABLESPOONS UNSALTED BUTTER

4 1/2 TABLESPOONS ALL-PURPOSE FLOUR

2 TEASPOONS DIJON MUSTARD, OR MORE
   TO TASTE

2 CUPS (8 OUNCES) GRATED EXTRA-
   SHARP WHITE CHEDDAR CHEESE, OR
   MORE TO TASTE

1/4 CUP GRATED PARMESAN CHEESE,
   PREFERABLY PARMIGIANO-REGGIANO,
   PLUS MORE FOR TOPPING

COARSE SALT, PREFERABLY KOSHER

8 OUNCES MACARONI, PREFERABLY
   CORKSCREW

1/2 CUP CRUSHED GARLIC CROUTONS,
   HOMEMADE (PAGE 62) OR PURCHASED

In a small, heavy-bottomed saucepan over medium heat, combine the whole milk, evaporated milk, garlic, bay leaf, allspice, red pepper flakes, and salt. Heat just to a boil and set aside.

Meanwhile, in another heavy saucepan, melt the butter over medium-low heat, add the flour, and whisk for 5 minutes. Do not brown. Remove from the heat.

Add 1 cup of the hot milk mixture to the flour mixture, and whisk into a thick paste. Continue to incorporate the milk, a cup at a time, whisking until smooth after each addition. When all the milk has been added, return the saucepan to the heat and cook over low to medium-low heat until somewhat thickened, about 15 minutes. Scrape the bottom frequently to avoid scorching. Turn off the heat and add the mustard, Cheddar cheese, and Parmesan cheese. Strain the sauce through a fine sieve, pressing and spreading it with a rubber spatula. Taste and adjust the seasoning with salt, mustard, and more cheese, if desired. (You can also increase the heat with a dash of Tabasco.)

Using plenty of boiling salted water, cook the macaroni at a rolling boil for 5 minutes. It should remain firm. Drain and combine it with half the cheese sauce. Turn the mixture into four to six 1-cup ramekins. The noodles should be soupy. If not, ladle more sauce over the noodles. (They will absorb a lot of sauce.) (The recipe can be made ahead to this point. Cool, cover, and refrigerate for up to 2 days.)

To serve, preheat the oven to 350°F. Top the noodles with the crushed croutons and Parmesan cheese and place on a baking sheet. Bake until hot throughout, about 25 minutes. To give a brown and bubbly finish, place the ramekins under the broiler, 4 inches from the heat, until the top is golden and bubbly, about 3 minutes. Serve immediately.

LINGUINE WITH GARLICKY CLAM SAUCE

Serves 4 as a first course, 2 as an entrée

Light and fresh tasting, this crowd-pleasing pasta dish is bright with the flavors of garlic, lemon, and parsley, and the minced clams add just the right texture and bite. The recipe is also quick to make and ideal for an impromptu meal, so keep a few extra cans of minced clams in the pantry just in case. You may find that the amount of clam juice varies from can to can, but don't worry: If you want more liquid, simply add extra wine.

3 CANS (6 OUNCES EACH) MINCED CLAMS
    WITH JUICE

1 TABLESPOON UNSALTED BUTTER

1 TABLESPOON OLIVE OIL

4 TO 6 LARGE GARLIC CLOVES, PRESSED

1/2 CUP WHITE WINE OR VERMOUTH

SCANT 1/2 TEASPOON DRIED OREGANO,
    CRUSHED

1/4 TEASPOON FRESHLY GROUND WHITE
    OR BLACK PEPPER

1 POUND DRIED LINGUINE

GRATED ZEST OF 1 SMALL LEMON

JUICE OF 1 SMALL LEMON

2 TO 3 TABLESPOONS CHOPPED, TENDER
    FLAT-LEAF PARSLEY

1/2 TEASPOON OR MORE COARSE SALT,
    PREFERABLY KOSHER, OR MORE
    TO TASTE

1/2 CUP GRATED PARMIGIANO-REGGIANO
    CHEESE (OPTIONAL)

FRESHLY GROUND PEPPER

Drain the cans of minced clams, reserving the clams and the juice separately.

In a medium-heavy skillet, melt the butter in the olive oil over medium-low heat. Add the garlic and sauté until fragrant and soft, 2 to 3 minutes. Do not let brown. Stir in the reserved clam juice, white wine, oregano, and the 1/4 teaspoon pepper. Bring the mixture to a boil, then reduce to a simmer and cook for 5 minutes. Stir in the reserved clams and cook until heated through.

Meanwhile, prepare the linguine according to package directions. Using plenty of boiling salted water, cook the linguine until al dente (tender but firm to the bite). (Serving hint: As the pasta water heats, place your serving bowl or platter over the pot to warm it.) Drain the linguine and transfer to a warm serving bowl or platter.

Stir the lemon zest, lemon juice, and parsley into the hot clam sauce, adding salt to taste. Immediately pour over the pasta and toss. Serve at once in warm, shallow bowls. At the table, pass the cheese, if desired, and season with salt and pepper to taste.

ROASTED GARLIC LASAGNA WITH FRESH SPINACH

Serves 10

This is my favorite lasagna recipe. The reason—besides the great flavor of roasted garlic? It's the fresh ricotta, which is far superior to the bland, mass-marketed variety. Seek it out at your neighborhood deli or gourmet shop, or in the specialty cheese section of your favorite supermarket. While you're filling your basket, look for another great find: packaged, ready-to-serve organic baby spinach. Triple-washed, crisp, and flavorful, it's a deluxe shortcut. + As with any lasagna, if you have time, assemble it a day ahead to let the flavors blend.

2 LARGE HEADS ROASTED GARLIC
    (2 1/2 TO 3 OUNCES EACH RAW)
    (SEE PAGE 14)
1 POUND RICOTTA CHEESE, PREFERABLY
    FRESH
2 CUPS LOOSELY PACKED FRESH BASIL
    LEAVES
COARSE SALT, PREFERABLY KOSHER, AND
    FRESHLY GROUND PEPPER
2 EGGS, LIGHTLY BEATEN
14 OUNCES DRIED CURLY-EDGED LASAGNA
    NOODLES
12 OUNCES YOUNG SPINACH LEAVES,
    TRIMMED OF ROOTS AND ANY TOUGH
    STEMS AND RINSED
6 1/2 TO 7 CUPS HOMEMADE OR PUR-
    CHASED SMOOTH MARINARA SAUCE,
    WITHOUT MEAT, SUCH AS POMI,
    DIVIDED
1 POUND MOZZARELLA CHEESE, GRATED
1/2 CUP GRATED PARMESAN CHEESE
1/2 CUP GRATED PECORINO ROMANO
    CHEESE

Squeeze the soft, golden garlic cloves out of their skins and coarsely chop. Transfer to a medium bowl, add the ricotta, and mix until blended. Stir in the basil and salt and pepper to taste. Stir in the eggs, mix until blended, and set aside.

In a large pot of salted boiling water, cook the noodles, 4 or 5 at a time, until flexible, about 10 minutes. Remove with a slotted spoon or tongs and plunge into cold water. When cool, lay flat on a clean dish towel to drain.

In a large saucepan over medium heat, add the spinach, along with any water left clinging to the leaves. Cover and cook, tossing the leaves with tongs, until wilted, 3 to 5 minutes. Drain in a sieve and press with the back of a spoon to release excess water. Coarsely chop and stir into the garlic ricotta mixture until blended.

To assemble, spread 1/2 cup marinara sauce on the bottom of a 13-by-9-by-2-inch baking pan. Arrange a layer of noodles over the sauce, running the noodles their full length in the pan. Spread one-third of the ricotta mixture over the noodles, then scatter with one-third of the mozzarella. Next, spread about 1 1/2 cups of marinara sauce over the grated cheese. Repeat this process 2 more times to create 3 layers of filling, pressing down lightly on the top layer of noodles to get everything to spread and settle before covering the final layer of noodles with the remaining marinara sauce. Sprinkle the Parmesan cheese and the pecorino romano cheese over the top. Cover the pan with foil, tenting slightly so the foil does not touch the lasagna. (The lasagna can be made up to 3 days ahead. Cool, cover, and refrigerate, or freeze for up to 3 months. Thaw in the refrigerator before baking.)

To bake, preheat the oven to 350°F. Punch a dozen small holes in the foil. Bake, covered with foil, until hot throughout, 35 to 40 minutes. If desired, remove the foil and run the pan under the broiler until the cheese is browned on top and bubbling hot. Let rest for 10 to 15 minutes before cutting into portions to serve.

GARLIC RISOTTO WITH BABY PEAS AND TRUFFLE OIL

Serves 4 as a first course, 2 as an entrée

Give me a little time, a glass of wine, and not too many ingredients, and I'll fix risotto. Homey, hearty, and satisfying, it makes an ideal entrée or side dish. This rendition makes a terrific informal supper with a simple green salad and a glass of smooth-bodied Italian Soave Classico. Garlic perfumes the entire dish, while the vermouth adds depth, the peas add color, taste, and texture, and the truffle oil—well, it's simply mesmerizing. + There's really no secret to great risotto, just a few self-evident truths: Use Italian Arborio rice, don't add too much liquid at one time (and not until the previous liquid has been nearly absorbed), and enjoy the simple act of stirring. You'll be rewarded.

1 TABLESPOON BUTTER

1 TABLESPOON OLIVE OIL

3 TO 4 LARGE GARLIC CLOVES, PRESSED

1 CUP ARBORIO RICE

1/2 CUP EXTRA-DRY VERMOUTH

4 CUPS CHICKEN BROTH, HEATED TO
    SIMMERING

1/2 CUP FRESH OR THAWED FROZEN
    BABY PEAS

1/4 CUP GRATED PARMESAN CHEESE

COARSE SALT, PREFERABLY KOSHER, AND
    FRESHLY GROUND PEPPER

TRUFFLE OIL FOR DRIZZLING (OR,
    IF UNAVAILABLE, VERY FRUITY
    OLIVE OIL)

In a medium-heavy skillet, melt the butter in the olive oil over medium heat. Add the garlic and sauté until fragrant, 1 to 2 minutes. Add the rice and continue to stir until the kernels are translucent and you can see the "eye" at the tip of the kernel. Do not let the rice or garlic brown.

Add the vermouth to the rice mixture, stirring the rice away from the bottom and sides of the pan until the liquid is nearly absorbed. Add the hot broth, 1/2 cup at a time, stirring constantly after each addition, until the liquid is nearly absorbed. Taste after 15 minutes to determine if the rice is firm to the bite. Stir in the peas and continue to add the hot broth, 1/2 cup at a time. Taste again after 5 minutes. The rice should be just tender to the bite.

Remove from the heat, stir in the cheese, and season with salt and pepper to taste. Mound the risotto into warmed shallow bowls, drizzle with truffle oil, and serve steaming hot. Alternatively, pass the truffle oil at the table.

RISOTTO-STUFFED TOMATOES

Serves 4 as a first course

These plump, luscious baked tomatoes feature risotto spiced up with Italian sausage, fresh basil, and a heady helping of garlic. They make an outstanding first course or side dish. Then again, double the recipe and use them as an entrée to serve with a big Caesar Salad (page 53), and your favorite red wine.

4 FIRM, MEDIUM TOMATOES (ABOUT
   8 OUNCES EACH)

5 OUNCES LEAN MILD ITALIAN SAUSAGE,
   CRUMBLED

1 TABLESPOON OLIVE OIL, PLUS MORE
   FOR DRIZZLING

4 TO 5 LARGE GARLIC CLOVES, MINCED
   (ABOUT 2 PACKED TABLESPOONS)

$1/2$ CUP ARBORIO RICE

$1/2$ CUP DRY VERMOUTH

$1^1/2$ CUPS VEGETABLE BROTH OR WATER,
   HEATED TO SIMMERING

$1/3$ CUP LOOSELY PACKED CHOPPED
   FRESH BASIL

COARSE SALT, PREFERABLY KOSHER, AND
   FRESHLY GROUND PEPPER

Preheat the oven to 400°F.

Remove the stems from the tomato tops and cut off the top third of each tomato, setting the tops aside. Using a small spoon, carefully scoop out the inner pulp without puncturing the walls of the tomatoes. Drain the pulp in a sieve placed over a bowl. (If desired, reserve the juice to substitute for some of the broth.) Arrange the scooped-out tomatoes in a medium baking dish so that they support one another. Set aside.

In a medium skillet, sauté the sausage in the olive oil over medium heat until it begins to turn from pink to brown. Stir in the garlic, lower the heat to medium, and continue to sauté until the garlic is fragrant and half the sausage is brown.

Stir in the rice and vermouth, stirring the rice away from the bottom and sides of the pan until the liquid is nearly absorbed. Add the hot broth, $1/2$ cup at a time, stirring constantly after each addition, until the liquid is nearly absorbed. Taste after 15 to 17 minutes to determine if the rice is firm to the bite. Remove from the heat, stir in the basil, and season with salt and pepper to taste.

Using clean kitchen scissors or a knife, snip or chop the reserved tomato pulp in the sieve, letting any remaining liquid drain into the bowl. Stir $1/3$ to $1/2$ cup of the pulp into the risotto and discard the rest with the drained liquid or save for other uses.

Spoon the filling into the prepared tomatoes (there may or may not be a little left over), and place the reserved tomato tops on the stuffed tomatoes. Drizzle a little olive oil over the tomatoes. Bake until the tomatoes are soft and browned and the rice is swollen, about 1 hour. Remove from the oven and cool in the cooking liquid for 10 minutes. With a large slotted spoon, carefully remove each tomato from the baking dish, and serve warm or at room temperature.

MEAT, POULTRY, AND SEAFOOD

Win flavor with the animal kingdom—add garlic!

GRILLED T-BONE STEAKS WITH GARLIC BOURBON BARBECUE SAUCE

Serves 4

I'm convinced that the best-tasting T-bones come from the grill. I'm not sure why. Maybe it's because my dad always cooked one on our overnight campouts. He'd grill the steak and let me choose which side of the bone was mine to eat: the tender oval tenderloin or the firmer top loin. Then, sitting by the fire, we'd dip our steaks into dad's tomatoey barbecue sauce (I'm still not sure how it got there). If our boxer Champ wasn't tagging along, I'd get the bone to nibble on too. Those were the days. + Dad loved bourbon, but I don't think he ever tried it in his barbecue sauce. He should have. It adds a matchless flavor, deep and slightly sweet. The bourbon seems to balance and blend the other robust ingredients, while the garlic adds a subtle background accent. + You'll notice that the recipe calls for both fresh and canned tomatoes. The fresh Roma tomatoes, baked to concentrate their flavors, add a bright, tangy note that's conspicuously missing without them. For a stronger salsa taste, don't simmer the sauce as directed; instead, use it straight from the processor.

SAUCE

12 OUNCES ROMA TOMATOES, CUT LENGTH-
    WISE INTO 1/4-INCH SLICES

1 CUP BOURBON

1 TABLESPOON PRESSED GARLIC (ABOUT
    3 LARGE CLOVES)

11/2 CUPS CANNED WHOLE PLUM TOMATOES,
    DRAINED AND PURÉED

1 TABLESPOON OLIVE OIL

3/4 TEASPOON WORCESTERSHIRE SAUCE

1 TABLESPOON PICKAPEPPA ORIGINAL
    SAUCE (NOT THE HOT ONE)

1 TEASPOON PACKED DARK BROWN SUGAR

1/2 TEASPOON KOSHER SALT

1 TO 2 TEASPOONS CHOPPED CANNED
    CHIPOTLE CHILIES (SEE NOTE)

4 T-BONE STEAKS, EACH 12 OUNCES AND
    1 INCH THICK, AT ROOM TEMPERATURE

KOSHER SALT AND FRESHLY GROUND
    PEPPER

TO MAKE THE SAUCE: Preheat the oven to 350°F. Oil a rimmed baking sheet and arrange the fresh tomato slices in a single layer. Bake until they shrivel and the edges are brown, 30 to 45 minutes.

Meanwhile, in a small saucepan, bring the bourbon to a boil over medium-high heat and reduce by half. Set aside.

In a food processor, combine the roasted tomatoes, the bourbon, garlic, canned tomatoes, olive oil, Worcestershire sauce, Pickapeppa sauce, brown sugar, salt, and 1 teaspoon chipotle, and process until smooth. Transfer to a saucepan and simmer for 5 minutes. Set aside to cool and let the flavors blend. Taste and adjust the seasoning with the remaining 1 teaspoon chipotle, if necessary.

TO PREPARE THE STEAKS: Season the steaks on each side with salt and pepper. Pour 1/2 cup of the bourbon sauce into a small bowl, and brush the steaks with the sauce. Let the meat rest while you prepare the grill. (Use some of the remaining sauce to brush the tops of the steaks during their last 5 minutes on the grill.)

Light a hot fire in a charcoal or gas grill. Before grilling, wipe the rack from back to front with a clean rag dipped in vegetable oil. Place the steaks on the hot rack and grill 4 to 6 minutes per side for medium-rare (about 145°F). Transfer the steaks to a platter and let rest for 5 minutes. Serve with the remaining sauce.

NOTE: If canned chipotle chilies are unavailable, substitute 3/4 teaspoon dried red chile flakes. The taste will be less smoky and will have a more peppery zest.

BEEF TENDERLOIN WITH PORT GARLIC SAUCE

Serves 2

This easy and elegant steak befits a special occasion. The glistening port sauce, made in a matter of minutes in the cast-iron skillet used to prepare the steak, is a velvety rich concoction with such a lavish taste and touch that you'll pause, close your eyes, and relish every spoonful. In this recipe, the garlic is minced to release its most flavorful oils and to complement the sweet intensity of the port.

2 BEEF TENDERLOIN FILETS,
EACH 6 TO 8 OUNCES AND 1 1/2 TO
2 INCHES THICK
COARSE SALT, PREFERABLY KOSHER, AND
FRESHLY GROUND PEPPER
2 TABLESPOONS OLIVE OIL
1 CUP PORT
2 TABLESPOONS BALSAMIC VINEGAR
1 LARGE GARLIC CLOVE, MINCED
(ABOUT 1 TEASPOON)
1 TABLESPOON UNSALTED BUTTER, CUT
INTO PIECES

Preheat the oven to 350°F. Lightly season the filets with salt and pepper and bring to room temperature.

In a 10-inch cast-iron skillet, heat the olive oil over medium-high heat for 1 minute. Fry the filets for 4 minutes per side. (To sear the edges, use tongs to hold and rotate the filets' edges against the hot skillet.)

Place the skillet and filets in the oven. For medium-rare, bake for 15 minutes, or until an instant-read thermometer inserted in the middle of a filet reaches 130°F to 135°F. Using a potholder to grasp the skillet's hot handle, remove it from the oven. Transfer the filets to a platter and let them rest, uncovered, for 5 to 7 minutes so the residual heat can finish the cooking (raising the filets' temperature to 135°F to 140°F).

Meanwhile, using a potholder, pour off the skillet drippings, reserving about 2 teaspoons in the skillet. Add the port and balsamic vinegar and bring to a boil, stirring constantly to scrape up the browned bits from the bottom. Cook until reduced by slightly more than half and a bit thickened. Remove from the heat, and immediately whisk in the garlic and butter until blended. To serve, arrange the steaks on plates and spoon a little sauce over each. At the table, pass additional sauce.

GRILLED LAMB CHOPS WITH GARLIC AND ROSEMARY

Serves 4

At a summertime barbecue, nothing could be more delectable than these superbly flavored marinated lamb chops—especially as part of a mixed grill that includes the marinated chicken breast variation and a few garlic sausages. Team them up with Garlic Mashed Potatoes My Way (page 111), Sautéed Spinach with Garlic and Lemon Zest (page 110), and Caesar Salad (page 53), and you have yourself a theme party. Now all that's missing is the Nervy, Heavenly Garlic Ice Cream. Ahhh, you'll find it here, too, on page 125.

6 LARGE GARLIC CLOVES, CUT IN HALF

2 TEASPOONS COARSE SALT, PREFERABLY KOSHER

1/2 CUP FRESH LEMON JUICE

1/2 CUP OLIVE OIL

1/4 CUP PEANUT OR VEGETABLE OIL

2 TEASPOONS FRESHLY GROUND PEPPER

1 TABLESPOON MINCED FRESH ROSE-MARY (ABOUT THREE 5-INCH SPRIGS)

8 LOIN LAMB CHOPS, EACH 6 TO 8 OUNCES AND 2 INCHES THICK

Sprinkle the garlic with the salt and mince, pressing the garlic into the salt with the flat of the knife to form a rough paste. Transfer to a jar with a lid. Add the lemon juice, olive oil, peanut oil, pepper, and rosemary, and shake vigorously. Set aside for 30 minutes. Shake again.

Arrange the chops in a large, nonreactive baking dish. Pour the marinade over the chops. Turn the chops to coat both sides, making sure some of the garlic and rosemary rests atop each chop. Marinate in the refrigerator, covered, turning once or twice, for 3 hours. (For a less pronounced flavor, 1 hour will do; for more garlicky goodness, marinate for up to 6 hours.) Remove 30 minutes before grilling.

Light a medium-high fire in a charcoal or gas grill. Before grilling, wipe the rack from back to front with a clean rag dipped in vegetable oil. Place the chops on the hot rack and grill 5 to 8 minutes per side for medium-rare (135°F to 140°F). To grill the edges, use tongs to hold the chops' edges against the grate. During the last 2 to 3 minutes, baste the chops with the marinade left in the baking dish. Transfer the chops to a platter and let rest for 5 minutes before serving.

VARIATION:

GRILLED CHICKEN WITH GARLIC AND ROSEMARY. Arrange a 3 1/2- to 4-pound cut-up chicken in a nonreactive baking dish and marinate in the refrigerator for 3 to 6 hours. Proceed as directed in the main recipe, placing the drumsticks and thighs skin-side down on the rack. Cook for 1 to 2 minutes per side. Next add the breast pieces, skin-side down. (Be careful of flareups caused by dripping fat. You may need to move pieces to a cooler spot to avoid burning.) Cook about 6 minutes, then turn them and continue grilling for 6 to 8 minutes. During the last 2 to 3 minutes, baste the chicken with the marinade left in the baking dish.

SHEPHERD'S PIE WITH GARLICKY MASHED POTATO CRUST

Serves 4

When life is hard, this homey English classic can soften the bumps. This is comfort food at its best. First your fork pierces a creamy layer of garlicky mashed potatoes, then it dives into a satisfying, stick-to-your-ribs filling of ground lamb, savory herbs, and garlic. When it reaches your mouth—oh my, it's satisfying. + In this recipe (as in most others), I prefer dried thyme to fresh. It's just too time-consuming to strip those tiny leaves off their stems. Since I make it a practice to refresh my jar of dried thyme every three or four months, I'm always sure of getting the flavor I want.

GARLICKY MASHED POTATOES

2 LARGE RUSSET POTATOES (ABOUT
    1^{1}/2 POUNDS) PEELED AND QUARTERED

2 TABLESPOONS UNSALTED BUTTER

^{1}/4 CUP REGULAR OR LIGHT SOUR CREAM

2 MEDIUM GARLIC CLOVES, PRESSED
    (ABOUT 1 TEASPOON)

LAMB FILLING

2 TABLESPOONS OLIVE OIL

1 MEDIUM TO LARGE ONION, CHOPPED

1 POUND GROUND LAMB

4 MEDIUM GARLIC CLOVES, MINCED
    (ABOUT 1 FIRMLY PACKED TABLESPOON)

1 TABLESPOON ALL-PURPOSE FLOUR

^{3}/4 CUP BEEF BROTH

1 TEASPOON DRIED THYME

1 TEASPOON CHOPPED FRESH OREGANO

1 TEASPOON CHOPPED FRESH ROSEMARY

PINCH OF GROUND NUTMEG

COARSE SALT, PREFERABLY KOSHER, AND
    FRESHLY GROUND PEPPER

OREGANO SPRIGS FOR GARNISHING
    (OPTIONAL)

TO PREPARE THE POTATOES: Put the potatoes in a large saucepan of salted water and bring to a boil over medium-high heat. Cook until tender, 15 to 20 minutes. Drain in a colander. Put the potatoes through a ricer or food mill placed over the saucepan. Add the butter, sour cream, and pressed garlic, and mix until smooth and fluffy. Set aside.

TO PREPARE THE LAMB FILLING: In a large skillet, heat the oil over medium heat and sauté the onion, stirring occasionally, for 10 minutes. Add the lamb, using a wooden spoon to break up the meat. Continue to sauté for 5 minutes. Stir in the minced garlic and continue to cook until the meat is browned. Drain off the fat.

Sprinkle the flour over the meat mixture and cook, stirring, for 2 minutes. Add the broth, thyme, chopped oregano, rosemary, and nutmeg. Bring to a boil, reduce the heat to a simmer, and cook for 10 minutes. Taste and adjust the seasoning with salt and pepper. Remove from the heat and let cool slightly.

TO ASSEMBLE THE PIE: Preheat the oven to 350°F.

Divide the lamb mixture among 4 single-serving ramekins, or place in a 9-inch baking dish. To create the crust, spread the mashed potatoes over the lamb, forming small peaks. Bake until the potatoes are flecked with brown, about 30 minutes. Garnish with oregano sprigs, if desired.

LAMB STEW WITH CARROTS AND NEW POTATOES

Serves 6

This hearty, flavorful mélange has everything you want in a stew, from the inviting aromas filling the house as the garlic, lamb, and rosemary simmer on the stove to the satisfying chunks of fork-tender lamb and vegetables. All the wonderful ingredients come together in the sauce, my favorite part of the stew. I dig into this dish with a fork, then I turn to a spoon, until finally I'm using a warm, crusty baguette to wipe up every last drop. This is home cooking at its best. + If you make this stew a day ahead, the flavors will have a chance to blend fully, but the garlic flavor may be less profound.

3 POUNDS BONELESS SHOULDER OR LEG OF
   LAMB, CUT INTO 1^{1}/2-INCH CUBES

^{1}/4 CUP OLIVE OIL

1 LARGE ONION, FINELY CHOPPED (ABOUT
   2 CUPS)

10 TO 12 MEDIUM TO LARGE GARLIC
   CLOVES, MINCED (ABOUT ^{1}/4 CUP)

^{1}/4 CUP ALL-PURPOSE FLOUR

4 CUPS CHICKEN BROTH

2 CUPS DRY VERMOUTH

JUICE OF 2 LEMONS

4 SPRIGS ROSEMARY, 4 TO 5 INCHES LONG

2 SMALL BAY LEAVES

2 TEASPOONS COARSE SALT, PREFERABLY
   KOSHER, OR MORE TO TASTE

2 TEASPOONS FRESHLY GROUND PEPPER,
   OR MORE TO TASTE

6 SLENDER BUNCH CARROTS, PEELED AND
   CUT INTO ^{1}/4-INCH DIAGONAL SLICES

24 SMALL RED POTATOES (12 TO
   16 OUNCES), CUT INTO QUARTERS

12 TO 16 PEARL ONIONS, PEELED AND LEFT
   WHOLE (OPTIONAL)

CHOPPED PARSLEY FOR GARNISHING

Remove any excess fat from the lamb. In a large Dutch oven, heat the olive oil over medium-high heat and lightly brown the lamb cubes. Using a slotted spoon, remove the lamb and set aside.

Sauté the onion and garlic until the onion is transparent. Reduce the heat to medium, add the flour, and stir until the flour picks up the residue in the bottom of the Dutch oven and forms a paste, 2 to 3 minutes. Slowly stir in the chicken broth, vermouth, lemon juice, rosemary sprigs, bay leaves, salt, and pepper.

Return the lamb cubes to the Dutch oven and bring the mixture to a boil. Simmer for 45 minutes. (At this point, you may wish to skim off any excess fat.) Add the carrots, potatoes, and pearl onions. Cover and cook until the lamb is tender and the vegetables are cooked through, 45 minutes to 1 hour. Remove the bay leaves and rosemary sprigs. Serve in deep plates and sprinkle with chopped parsley.

GRILLED GARLIC SAUSAGES WITH RATATOUILLE AND SOFT GORGONZOLA POLENTA

Serves 4

For this delectable dish, thanks go to Randall Cronwell, the creative chef behind some of the best garlic sausage in Portland, Oregon. The recipe is part of a late-harvest menu he created for an article I wrote about him for our local newspaper, *The Oregonian*. The menu begins with a Bibb lettuce salad dressed with a champagne vinaigrette and ends with a warm, mixed berry compote topped with vanilla ice cream. To complete the meal, Cronwell serves a Zinfandel or rioja wine, and we're all the better for it.

4 TO 6 GARLIC SAUSAGES

RATATOUILLE

1 MEDIUM ZUCCHINI, CUT INTO 1/4- TO
   1/2-INCH DICE

2 SMALL JAPANESE EGGPLANTS, CUT INTO
   1/4- TO 1/2-INCH DICE

1 HEAPING TABLESPOON FINELY CHOPPED
   FRESH BASIL

1 HEAPING TABLESPOON FINELY CHOPPED
   FRESH OREGANO

3 TABLESPOONS OLIVE OIL, DIVIDED

1 SMALL RED ONION, CUT INTO 1/4- TO
   1/2-INCH DICE

1 SMALL RED BELL PEPPER, CORED, SEEDED,
   AND CUT INTO 1/4- TO 1/2-INCH DICE

1 SMALL YELLOW BELL PEPPER, CORED,
   SEEDED, AND CUT INTO 1/4- TO 1/2-INCH
   DICE

4 LARGE GARLIC CLOVES, MINCED (ABOUT
   2 FIRMLY PACKED TABLESPOONS)

1 MEDIUM TOMATO, PEELED AND CHOPPED

DASH OF RED WINE VINEGAR

COARSE SALT, PREFERABLY KOSHER, AND
   FRESHLY GROUND PEPPER

TO COOK THE SAUSAGES: Prick each sausage in 4 to 6 places. Arrange the sausages in a sauté pan large enough to hold them in a single layer, cover with water, and bring to a simmer. Poach the sausages until half-cooked, 4 to 5 minutes. Transfer to a wire rack and drain on paper towels. (If you decide to omit grilling the sausages, continue poaching until cooked through, 8 to 10 minutes.)

Light a medium-high fire in a charcoal or gas grill. Before grilling, wipe the rack from back to front with a clean rag dipped in vegetable oil. Lightly brush the sausages with oil and place on the hot rack. Grill the sausages until the casings are browned and crisp and the meat is cooked through, 4 to 6 minutes per side. Be careful of flareups caused by the dripping fat. When this happens, move the sausages to another section of the grill to avoid burning until the flames die. (If you omit poaching the sausages first, grill them for 7 to 10 minutes per side.)

TO MAKE THE RATATOUILLE: In a bowl, toss the zucchini, eggplants, basil, and oregano in 2 tablespoons of the olive oil, and set aside. In a sauté pan, heat the remaining 1 tablespoon olive oil over medium-high heat. Sauté the onion and bell peppers for 1 minute. Add the eggplant mixture and the garlic and sauté, stirring constantly, for 2 to 3 minutes. Add the tomato and toss. Add the vinegar and toss. Remove from the heat and add salt and pepper to taste.

CONTINUED

POLENTA

4 1/2 CUPS SALTED WATER, DIVIDED

1 1/2 CUPS QUICK-COOKING POLENTA

5 OUNCES TRIMMED, SOFT, SWEET
  GORGONZOLA CHEESE, DIVIDED INTO
  SMALL CHUNKS

1/4 CUP (1/2 STICK) UNSALTED BUTTER,
  CUT INTO PIECES

COARSE SALT, PREFERABLY KOSHER,
  AND FRESHLY GROUND PEPPER

FRESH BASIL LEAVES FOR GARNISHING

TO MAKE THE POLENTA: In a medium, heavy-bottomed saucepan, bring 4 cups of the salted water to a boil. Add the polenta in a slow, steady stream, whisking constantly. Reduce the heat to low and simmer, whisking constantly, until the polenta thickens. At the 3-minute point, add the remaining 1/2 cup water and continue to stir until the polenta pulls away from the sides of the pan, 4 to 6 minutes. Remove from the heat and stir in the cheese and butter until melted. The polenta should resemble a thick soup. Taste and season with salt and pepper.

To serve, pour the polenta onto individual plates. Cut the sausages into 1/2-inch diagonal slices. Arrange the sausage slices along the outside edges of the polenta. Spoon the ratatouille over the center of each polenta serving. Garnish with basil leaves and serve.

GARLIC-STUDDED ROAST PORK LOIN WITH MOJO

Serves 4 to 6

Pork loves garlic, so a garlic-lover's quest is to find delicious ways to serve it. In this Cuban-style recipe, the roast is studded with oregano- and cumin-seasoned garlic slivers that carry their flavor deep into the meat. The outside of the loin is also coated with the herbs, making it fragrant and flavorful and just right for serving with a citrusy mojo (pronounced "mo-ho") or table sauce. Traditionally served over pit-roasted pork, mojo works wonders on other grilled meats or roasted tiny new potatoes. (When the winter blahs descend, one of my favorite appetizers or snacks by the fire is a bowl of this mojo surrounded by tiny, warm-from-the-oven potatoes. *Viva el mojo!*) + This recipe is also an excellent brunch or buffet item. Cook the pork a day ahead, freeze, and then take it to the butcher to be thinly sliced (the freezing makes it easier to slice). Served with 2-inch bakery rolls and a bowl of mojo for drizzling, you've got great bite-size sandwiches for 10 to 12 guests.

MOJO

2 1/2 TABLESPOONS CHOPPED GARLIC
(ABOUT 6 MEDIUM CLOVES)

1/2 TEASPOON FIRMLY PACKED GRATED
LIME ZEST

3 TABLESPOONS FRESH LIME JUICE

1/4 TEASPOON FIRMLY PACKED GRATED
ORANGE ZEST

2 TABLESPOONS FRESH ORANGE JUICE

3/4 TEASPOON GROUND CUMIN

1/2 TEASPOON KOSHER SALT

1/2 CUP EXTRA-VIRGIN OLIVE OIL

FRESHLY GROUND PEPPER

1 TABLESPOON MINCED CILANTRO

PORK

1 PORK TENDERLOIN (ABOUT 2 POUNDS)

2 TEASPOONS DRIED OREGANO

1/2 TEASPOON GROUND CUMIN

1/2 TEASPOON KOSHER SALT

1/2 TEASPOON FRESHLY GROUND PEPPER

2 TO 3 MEDIUM GARLIC CLOVES, CUT
INTO SLIVERS

TO MAKE THE MOJO: In a blender, blend the garlic, lime zest, lime juice, orange zest, orange juice, cumin, and salt until the garlic is finely chopped. With the machine running, slowly add the oil in a thin stream until emulsified. Transfer to a bowl, season to taste with pepper, and stir in the cilantro. Makes 3/4 cup. (The mojo can be made up to 4 days ahead. Cover and refrigerate if you make it in advance.)

TO PREPARE THE PORK: If necessary, fold the tenderloin's narrow ends back over themselves, toward the center, to make the tenderloin an even width throughout; secure with kitchen twine.

In a small bowl, combine the oregano, cumin, salt, and pepper. Using a mortar or the back of a spoon, stir and crush together the ingredients until the oregano is well crushed. Toss the garlic slivers in the spice mixture. Using the point of a paring knife, poke deep slits in the roast and insert the garlic slivers. Rub the remaining spice mixture over the meat. Wrap the roast in foil and refrigerate for at least 2 hours or overnight.

Preheat the oven to 475°F. Arrange the oven rack in the center of the oven.

Take the meat from the refrigerator, unwrap, and place it on a rack in a roasting pan. Roast for 20 minutes, or until an instant-read thermometer, inserted into the middle of the thickest end of the pork, reads 140°F to 145°F. Remove and let the roast rest, uncovered, for 5 minutes. (The residual heat will raise the meat's internal temperature another 5 degrees.) To serve, cut into 1/2-inch slices and serve accompanied by a bowl of the sauce.

FORTY-CLOVES-AND-WHO'S-COUNTING CHICKEN

Serves 4

It's doing the simple things well and using good ingredients that create the best flavor and taste. This dish proves it. A free-range organic chicken, lots of garlic, fresh herbs, and extra-virgin olive oil produce a dish with superb flavor, a juicy texture, and an unforgettable aroma. In the traditional Provençal dish, the chicken is roasted in a tightly covered Dutch oven. But I prefer this method, which lightly browns the chicken and caramelizes the garlic cloves, making them ever so tasty when eaten whole or seasoned with salt and pepper.

46 PLUMP, UNPEELED GARLIC CLOVES, DIVIDED

1 1/2 TEASPOONS OR MORE COARSE SALT, PREFERABLY KOSHER

ABOUT 1/2 CUP COARSELY CHOPPED FRESH HERBS, SUCH AS TARRAGON, THYME, OREGANO, AND SAGE

FRESHLY GROUND PEPPER

1/4 CUP PLUS 2 TABLESPOONS EXTRA-VIRGIN OLIVE OIL

1 ORGANIC FREE-RANGE FRYER (3 1/2 TO 4 POUNDS), CUT-UP

THINLY SLICED FRENCH BREAD OR TOAST, HEATED, FOR SERVING

Preheat the oven to 400°F.

Peel 6 of the garlic cloves, sprinkle with salt, and mince, pressing the garlic into the salt with the flat of the knife to form a rough paste. Transfer to a small bowl and stir in the chopped herbs, pepper, and the 1/4 cup olive oil.

With clean fingers, generously spread the garlic mixture over the chicken pieces. Set the pieces in a roasting pan with the breast sides up. Add the 40 unpeeled cloves to the bowl that contained the garlic mixture and toss to lightly coat them with the oil remaining on the sides of the bowl. Tuck the garlic cloves in and around the chicken pieces. Drizzle the remaining 2 tablespoons of olive oil over the chicken. Roast for 30 minutes and then drizzle the chicken with the pan juices. Continue to roast until fork-tender and just browned, 45 minutes to 1 hour, or until an instant-read thermometer inserted in the middle of a breast reads 165°F.

Serve the chicken with the pan juices and garlic cloves. Pass the French bread. Squeeze the softer roasted garlic from the root end onto the bread, spread, and enjoy with the chicken. Squeeze or pop the more caramelized garlic from the root end onto the plate and eat whole, seasoned with salt and pepper.

THAI CHICKEN AND NOODLES WITH GARLIC, GINGER, AND ROASTED PEANUTS

Serves 2

This is one of those splendid, Asian-style dishes that improve your mood with every crunchy bite. Once the mincing and chopping are behind you, the dish goes together with a quick sauté. Brimming with color and alive with fragrance, it's a marvelous meal to indulge your love of garlic and other healthful vegetables. (If this is a last-minute deal, feel free to vary the vegetables, so long as you keep the garlic.)

6 TO 8 OUNCES BONELESS, SKINLESS CHICKEN BREAST, JULIENNED (SEE NOTE)

3 TEASPOONS ASIAN SESAME OIL, DIVIDED

1/4 CUP FISH SAUCE

3 TABLESPOONS FRESH LIME JUICE

2 TEASPOONS CORNSTARCH

6 OUNCES CHINESE-STYLE NOODLES

3 TEASPOONS PEANUT OIL, DIVIDED

2/3 CUP SLICED FRESH MUSHROOMS

1/3 CUP THINLY SLICED RED ONION

6 TO 8 GREEN ONIONS, BOTH WHITE AND GREEN PARTS, CUT INTO 1-INCH SEGMENTS

1/2 SMALL RED OR ORANGE BELL PEPPER, SEEDED AND JULIENNED (SEE NOTE)

1/2 CUP SLICED SUGAR SNAP PEAS

1 MEDIUM JALAPEÑO PEPPER, SEEDED AND JULIENNED (SEE NOTE)

1 PIECE (1 BY 2 INCHES, 3/4 OUNCE) FRESH GINGER, PEELED AND JULIENNED

6 MEDIUM TO LARGE GARLIC CLOVES, MINCED

1/3 CUP BASIL LEAVES, PREFERABLY THAI, JULIENNED (SEE NOTE)

1/3 CUP FRESH WHOLE CILANTRO LEAVES

1/3 CUP CHOPPED UNSALTED ROASTED PEANUTS

In a small bowl, toss together the chicken and 2 teaspoons of the sesame oil. Set aside at room temperature.

In a small bowl or cup, mix together the fish sauce, lime juice, and cornstarch. Set aside.

Prepare the noodles according to the package directions. Using plenty of boiling salted water, cook the noodles until they float to the top, about 5 minutes. Drain and transfer to a warm serving bowl.

In a large, heavy skillet, heat 2 teaspoons of the peanut oil over medium-high heat until hot. (To test, add a piece of chicken to the hot oil. When it sizzles, the temperature is right.) Add the chicken, stir, and turn to separate and cook. When the chicken is a uniform color, transfer with the juices to the noodle bowl.

In the skillet used to cook the chicken, heat the remaining 1 teaspoon of peanut oil, add the mushrooms, and sauté briefly. Turn the heat up to high, add the red onion, green onion, red bell pepper, snap peas, jalapeño, and remaining 1 teaspoon of sesame oil and stir briefly. Add the ginger and garlic and stir constantly. Turn the heat down to medium, add the fish sauce mixture, and cook, stirring constantly, for 1 to 2 minutes.

Add the vegetables to the noodle bowl, and toss. Add the basil, cilantro, and half of the peanuts, and lightly toss. Sprinkle the remaining peanuts over the top and serve at once.

NOTE: To julienne chicken or vegetables, cut into matchstick-size pieces, about 1/8 inch thick and 2 inches long. To julienne herbs, stack the leaves, roll into a tight cylinder, and slice thinly to produce ribbons.

PAN-ROASTED SEAFOOD WITH SMOKY PAPRIKA AND ROASTED GARLIC

Serves 4 to 6 as an appetizer, 2 as an entrée

On cold winter evenings when all you want to do is sit cuddled up with a rich, easy-to-fix meal, this is the one to choose. Chock-full of fresh seafood, its heady broth is energized by smoky paprika that begs for a spoon or a chunk of bread to get every last drop. Golden cloves of mellow, roasted garlic stud the dish and add a creamy richness. There's no need for butter or whipping cream to sabotage this recipe's healthful appeal. Created by Oregon chef (and dedicated runner) Eric Laslow, this is a marathon meal of great tastes and good flavors.

3 LARGE HEADS ROASTED GARLIC
(2 1/2 TO 3 OUNCE EACH RAW)
(SEE PAGE 14)

2 TABLESPOONS EXTRA-VIRGIN OLIVE OIL,
PLUS MORE FOR DRIZZLING

12 TO 14 FINGERLING POTATOES
(8 OUNCES TOTAL), PARBOILED FOR
5 MINUTES AND CUT INTO 1/2-INCH
SLICES

4 LARGE, FRESH SEA SCALLOPS

COARSE SALT, PREFERABLY KOSHER, AND
FRESHLY GROUND PEPPER

1/4 SMALL FENNEL BULB, CORED AND
SLICED

PINCH OF DRIED RED PEPPER FLAKES

6 FRESH MUSSELS, SCRUBBED, WITH
BEARDS REMOVED

4 JUMBO SHRIMP, PEELED AND DEVEINED

6 FRESH CLAMS, SCRUBBED

1/4 TEASPOON PLUS A PINCH OF SMOKED
PAPRIKA

1/4 CUP WHITE WINE

1 TABLESPOON CHOPPED FLAT-LEAF
PARSLEY

GRILLED CRUSTY RUSTIC BREAD

When the roasted garlic is cool enough to handle, squeeze the soft cloves out of their skins and set aside. Preheat the oven to 425°F.

In a large, ovenproof skillet, heat the oil over medium-high heat. Season the potatoes and scallops with salt and pepper and distribute in the pan in a single layer. Add the fennel, red pepper flakes, and roasted garlic cloves and sauté until the scallops brown slightly on one side, about 2 minutes.

Add the mussels, shrimp, and clams. Season with the paprika. Bake in the lower third of the oven until the mussels and clams open, 15 to 20 minutes. Check after 10 minutes and continue to roast until they are done. If any of the shellfish remain closed, discard them. Return the skillet to the stovetop, stir in the white wine and parsley, and simmer for 1 minute. Ladle into warm, shallow bowls. Drizzle with olive oil, and serve with grilled, crusty bread.

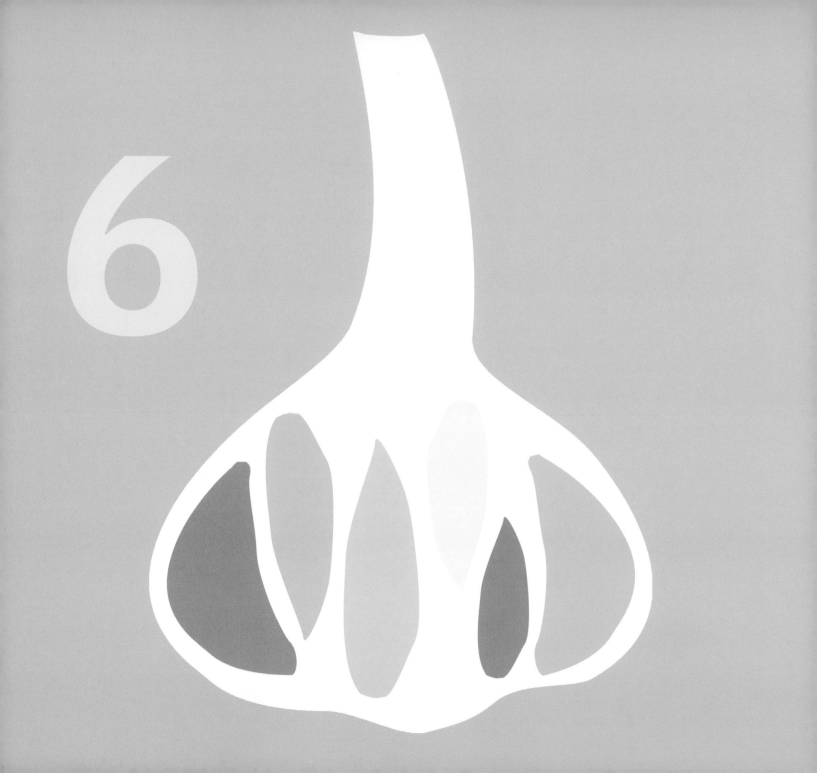

VEGETABLES THAT SHOUT AND SING

Side dishes fine-tuned with garlic

GRILLED CORN ON THE COB WITH FESTIVAL GARLIC BUTTER

Serves 4

Grilled corn on the cob is one of summer's finest pleasures, and it's even more flavorful when it's lightly caramelized with sweetened garlic butter. (If the Gilroy Garlic Festival can butter its kettle popcorn this way, think how delicious the topping can be on fresh, plump corn kernels.) + When stalking a great ear of corn, look for green husks, firm kernels (hey, rather than tearing back the husk, you can squeeze the ear right through it), and golden, slightly sticky tassels. It's worth the hunt.

1/4 CUP SUGAR

1 TABLESPOON WATER

2 TABLESPOONS UNSALTED BUTTER

4 LARGE GARLIC CLOVES, PRESSED
   (1 1/2 TO 2 TEASPOONS)

4 LARGE EARS FRESH CORN, HUSKED

In a small saucepan, combine the sugar and water over medium-low heat and stir until most of the sugar dissolves. Add the butter and the garlic and continue to heat, stirring, until the butter melts and the mixture is hot but not boiling. Set aside to cool until warm. The mixture will be thick and cloudy.

Place the ears of corn on a baking sheet. Brush the corn all over with the butter mixture. (You can do this up to 4 hours ahead, cover the corn, and set it aside.)

Light a medium-high fire in a charcoal or gas grill. Before grilling, wipe the rack from back to front with a clean rag dipped in vegetable oil. (If you go from front to back, you might lose some hair on your arm.) Grill the corn until lightly charred in spots, 6 to 8 minutes, turning frequently. Serve at once.

GREEN BEANS WITH GARLIC

Serves 4

According to my tastes, there are never enough ways to fix or to eat green beans. My daughter Julie—well, that's a different story. Let's just say that this is the only way she'll eat them. She says, "Mom, you're right. Everything does taste better with garlic, *even* green beans." Who knows, with this recipe, you just might make a vegetable eater out of someone you love! + To make sure your beans are fresh and at their best, pick one up and break it in two. It should snap crisply. If you find the fibrous "string" that edges many bean varieties, you'll need to remove the strings from all the beans.

¼ CUP GARLIC CROUTONS FOR ONE AND
ALL (YOUR CHOICE, PAGES 62–64),
CRUSHED TO CRUMBS OR PURCHASED
CROUTONS
1 TABLESPOON GRATED PARMESAN OR
ROMANO CHEESE
1 POUND FRESH GREEN BEANS, ENDS
REMOVED AND SNAPPED IN HALF IF
LARGE
4 MEDIUM GARLIC CLOVES, MINCED
(1 FIRMLY PACKED TABLESPOON)
2 TABLESPOONS EXTRA-VIRGIN OLIVE OIL
COARSE SALT, PREFERABLY KOSHER, AND
FRESHLY GROUND PEPPER

In a small bowl, mix together the crouton crumbs and cheese and set aside.

Bring a large pot of salted water to a brisk boil. Add the beans and boil until they are almost tender and their color deepens, 5 to 8 minutes. (After 5 minutes, check a bean for doneness.) Drain and rinse in cold water to stop cooking.

In a large skillet, sauté the garlic in the olive oil over medium-high heat, stirring frequently, until the garlic is fragrant and translucent, about 1½ minutes. Add the cooked beans, and sauté for 1 to 2 minutes. Remove from the heat. Taste and adjust the seasoning with the salt and pepper. Transfer to a serving dish, sprinkle with the reserved crouton mixture, and serve.

VARIATION:

For an Italian twist, try **GREEN BEANS WITH GARLIC, PINE NUTS, AND GOLDEN RAISINS.** Follow the main recipe, adding ¼ cup pine nuts and ¼ cup golden raisins to the cooked green beans for the final sauté.

SAUTÉED SPINACH WITH GARLIC AND LEMON ZEST

Serves 2

What makes sautéed spinach so good? Fresh, young leaves. What makes sautéed spinach great? Lots of garlic and a little lemon zest. Isn't it nice that it's good for you too? + For a subtle garlic taste, after sautéing the garlic slices in the olive oil, discard them. For more flavor, add them back just before serving.

2 TABLESPOONS OLIVE OIL, PLUS MORE
   FOR DRIZZLING
2 LARGE GARLIC CLOVES, HAND-CUT
   CROSSWISE INTO THIN SLICES
   (1 MOUNDED TABLESPOON)
6 CUPS FRESH, YOUNG FLAT-LEAF
   SPINACH LEAVES (8 OUNCES)
   (SEE NOTE)
COARSE SALT, PREFERABLY KOSHER, AND
   FRESHLY GROUND PEPPER
1/4 TEASPOON GRATED LEMON ZEST

In a large skillet, heat the oil over medium heat. Add the garlic and cook, shaking the pan, until light golden brown, about 3 minutes. Remove and reserve the garlic. Raise the heat to high and, using tongs, add the spinach and a dash of salt and pepper. Toss, sprinkle in the lemon zest, and continue to cook, tossing, until barely wilted and glossy green, about 2 minutes. Remove from the heat and, using tongs, transfer the spinach to a colander. Gently squeeze the spinach to release excess water. Return to the skillet, add the reserved garlic, if desired, and drizzle with olive oil. Taste and adjust the seasoning with salt and pepper. Serve immediately.

NOTE: Packaged, triple-washed, organic baby spinach can be found in the produce departments of most supermarkets.

GARLIC MASHED POTATOES MY WAY

Serves 4 to 6

When it comes to mashed potatoes my way, there are a few simple rules: namely, garlic, cream, and butter in good supply. This is one of those times when calories don't count and flavor is all that matters. (To cut calories, you could use chicken broth or one of those milks that border on blue glaze, but why?) + Like my mother, I peel and quarter the potatoes before they're cooked, even though there is something to be said for boiling potatoes with their skins on. Many mashed-potato enthusiasts believe the skins keep the flesh from getting soggy so they're able to absorb more melted butter, cream, and garlic. Either way is fine. + In this recipe, a food mill creates mashed potatoes that are smooth and cloudlike. For a smashed spud look, use some muscle and the back of a large spoon.

6 TABLESPOONS UNSALTED BUTTER

4 TO 6 LARGE GARLIC CLOVES, SLICED
    (ABOUT 1/4 CUP)

2 POUNDS RUSSET OR YUKON GOLD
    POTATOES, PEELED AND QUARTERED

2 TABLESPOONS COARSE SALT,
    PREFERABLY KOSHER, OR MORE
    TO TASTE

1/4 TO 1/2 CUP HEAVY (WHIPPING) CREAM
    OR HALF-AND-HALF

FRESHLY GROUND PEPPER (OPTIONAL)

In a small saucepan, melt the butter over low heat. Add the garlic, making sure the pieces are covered with the butter. Keeping the heat as low as possible, cook the garlic, stirring occasionally at first and continuously as the oil heats, until the garlic is tender and the air is fragrant with garlic, 8 to 10 minutes. Do not let the garlic brown. Remove from the heat and set aside.

Meanwhile, in a large saucepan, cover the potatoes with cold water. Bring to a boil over medium-high heat. Add the salt, reduce the heat to a simmer, and cook until the potatoes are tender, 15 to 20 minutes. Drain in a colander for 1 minute, letting the steam rise and the potatoes dry out.

Meanwhile, using a slotted spoon, separate the garlic from the butter, reserving the butter. Put the potatoes and garlic through a ricer or food mill placed over a large bowl or the saucepan. Add the warm butter and mix until smooth. Stir 1/4 cup cream into the potatoes until smooth. Drizzle in the remaining 1/4 cup cream, 1 tablespoon at a time, until the potatoes reach the desired consistency. Taste and adjust the seasoning with salt and pepper, if desired. Serve at once.

CRISPY GARLIC POTATO CHIPS

Serves 4 to 6

Next time the gang stops by, skip the fancy appetizers and make something easy that everyone will love—warm, crispy potato chips flush with garlic. They're a cinch to make and don't even require peeling or double frying. What are you waiting for? + The one kitchen tool that guarantees success here is a mandoline. It creates paper-thin slices in no time flat. Until recently, it was a major kitchen investment—to the tune of $100 or more. Now most kitchen stores carry models under $20 that work just fine. If you don't have or want one, depend on a good chef's knife and a steady hand.

VEGETABLE OIL FOR FRYING

2 POUNDS MEDIUM RUSSET POTATOES,
    UNPEELED

8 TO 10 LARGE GARLIC CLOVES, THINLY
    SLICED

GARLIC SALT OR COARSE SALT,
    PREFERABLY KOSHER

In a deep, heavy-bottomed pot or wok, heat 3 to 4 inches of oil over medium heat.

Meanwhile, using a mandoline, cut the potatoes crosswise into the thinnest slices possible. (If you don't have a mandoline, use a sharp chef's knife.)

When the oil begins to shimmer (about 350°F on a candy thermometer), drop the garlic slices into the oil and cook until just golden, 30 to 45 seconds. Using a small fine-mesh sieve, remove the garlic and drain on paper towels. When cool, crumble into a small bowl, and set aside.

In small batches, add the potato slices to the hot oil, cooking until golden brown and crisp, 4 to 8 minutes. (The time will vary, depending on the thickness of the slices.) Using a slotted spoon, remove the chips and drain on several layers of paper towels. Immediately sprinkle each batch with crumbled garlic and a generous amount of garlic salt. Nibble as you make them or, after the last batch is seasoned, serve immediately while still warm.

ROASTED GREEK POTATOES WITH GARLIC, LEMON, AND OREGANO

Serves 4

These flavorful roast potatoes go well with practically any meat dish they accompany. One reason is because this recipe uses russet, or baking, potatoes, which are high in starch and soak up all the juices created from the mingling of garlic, oregano, lemon juice, olive oil, and broth. + For a main dish meal, I'll brown boneless chicken cutlets and slip them in with the potatoes. With some crusty bread for dipping and a Greek salad, life is good.

6 LARGE GARLIC CLOVES, CUT IN HALF

1 TEASPOON COARSE SALT, PREFERABLY
   KOSHER, PLUS MORE TO TASTE

1/2 CUP EXTRA-VIRGIN OLIVE OIL

3 POUNDS RUSSET POTATOES, PEELED
   AND CUT INTO 1 1/2-INCH CHUNKS

1 1/2 TEASPOONS DRIED OREGANO

1/2 CUP CHICKEN BROTH

1/4 CUP FRESH LEMON JUICE

FRESHLY GROUND PEPPER

Preheat the oven to 400°F.

Sprinkle the garlic with salt and mince, pressing the garlic into the salt with the flat of the knife to form a rough paste. Transfer to a 13-by-9-by-2-inch baking dish and drizzle with the olive oil. Add the potatoes, sprinkle with oregano, toss well to coat, and arrange in the dish in a single layer. Bake for 15 minutes. Add the broth, toss, and continue to bake for 10 minutes. Drizzle the lemon juice over the potatoes, toss, and continue to bake until the potatoes are cooked through, about 15 minutes. Serve at once. At the table, season with salt and pepper.

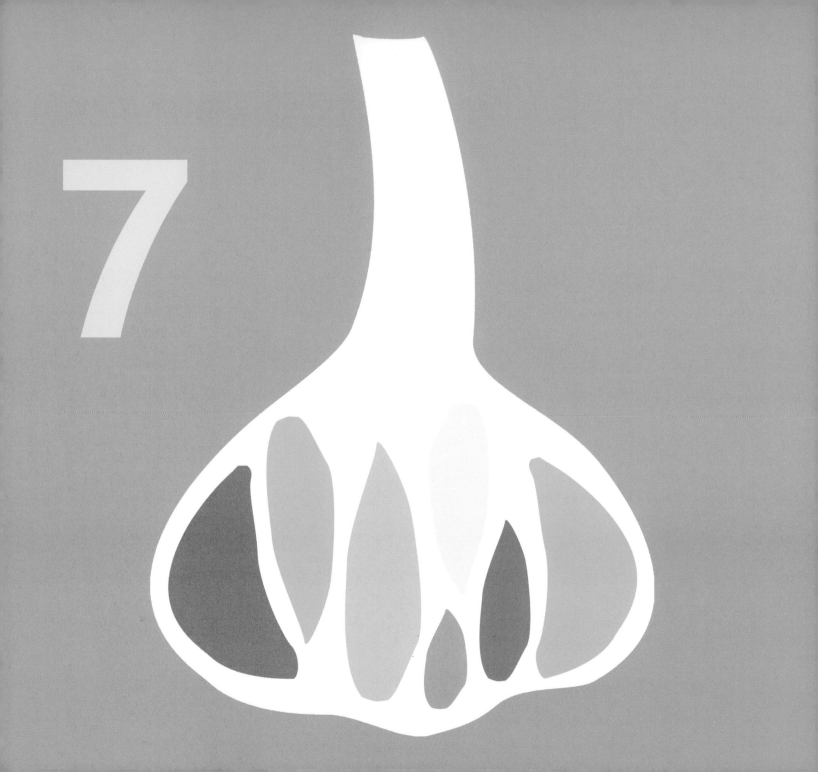

ESSENTIAL GARLIC FLAVOR BOOSTERS

Savory ways to tantalize tastebuds

GOLDEN GARLIC, ONION, AND SHALLOT MARMALADE

Makes about 1¹/₄ cups

From topping a just-grilled burger to crowning bite-size hors d'oeuvres, this condiment will impress you with its versatility. One of my favorite taste-tempting *amuse-bouches,* or mini-appetizers, is a **GOLDEN TEARDROP TARTLET.** I simply purchase tiny frozen phyllo tartlet shells found in the supermarket and bake them according to the directions. Then I fill each one with a teaspoon or two of marmalade, and I'm ready to party. + A word to the wise: Use a sharp chef's knife to help you with the prep work. Also, don't take any shortcuts. Have the garlic and shallots sliced before you begin to cook the onions. Believe me, it takes a while to peel and thinly slice them—and it takes even longer if your knife is dull. Also be sure to use a large skillet; a small one makes it more difficult to cook away the water from the onions.

1¹/₂ TABLESPOONS UNSALTED BUTTER

3 HEADS GARLIC (7 TO 9 OUNCES),
    SEPARATED INTO CLOVES, PEELED,
    AND THINLY SLICED

3 TO 4 SMALL YELLOW ONIONS (ABOUT
    1 POUND), THINLY SLICED

8 SHALLOTS (ABOUT 9 OUNCES), THINLY
    SLICED

¹/₂ CUP DRY WHITE WINE

¹/₂ TEASPOON SUGAR

COARSE SALT, PREFERABLY KOSHER, AND
    FRESHLY GROUND PEPPER

In a large, heavy skillet, melt the butter over medium heat. Add the garlic, onions, and shallots, stirring until they are coated with butter. Stir in the wine. Reduce the heat to low, cover, and cook, stirring occasionally, until the mixture is reduced by two-thirds and the onions are very soft, about 1¹/₂ hours. Uncover and continue to cook, stirring often, until the liquid is almost gone, about 15 minutes. Sprinkle the sugar over the garlic mixture and stir constantly until golden brown, about 10 minutes. Remove from the heat and season with salt and pepper to taste. Serve hot or at room temperature. Store in an airtight container in the refrigerator for up to 1 week.

GREMOLATA

Makes $1/2$ cup

Gremolata is the impressive garnish traditionally sprinkled over braised veal shanks in the Italian dish called osso buco. It is a simple, vivid mixture of minced fresh garlic, parsley, and lemon zest. In this version by Jane Zwinger, a small amount of olive oil is added to bind the mixture as well as to blend and mellow the flavors. Use it as a lively finishing touch to any braised meat or hearty stew.

2 LARGE GARLIC CLOVES, CHOPPED
(1 TABLESPOON PLUS 1 TEASPOON
FIRMLY PACKED)

$3/4$ CUP PACKED FLAT-LEAF PARSLEY
LEAVES

GRATED ZEST FROM 2 LARGE LEMONS
(ABOUT 2 TABLESPOONS)

$1/4$ TEASPOON COARSE SALT, PREFERABLY
KOSHER

1 TABLESPOON EXTRA-VIRGIN OLIVE OIL

In a mini-prep processor, pulse the garlic and parsley until minced. Add the lemon zest, salt, and olive oil and pulse until combined. For best flavor, use within several hours.

AS-YOU-LIKE-IT PESTOS

Pesto is one of the essential garlic flavor boosters. It's fresh, assertive, and irresistible on pastas and practically every other savory food it touches. In the summer, freshly made, it gives pizzazz to grilled meats, chicken, fish, and vegetables. With pesto in the freezer, you can flavor winter's hearty soups and stews, even salad dressings, with the fragrance of summer. + Another great thing about pesto is that you can vary and adapt the recipe to suit your tastes. While pine nuts are traditional, you may prefer the stronger taste of walnuts. When it comes to the cheese, even though Parmigiano-Reggiano is the one often used, other hard Italian cheeses also are good (I often substitute pecorino romano). If you like your pesto thinner, simply add more oil or, if you're using it on pasta, add a little of the pasta's cooking water. + If you're planning to freeze the pesto, leave the cheese out until you thaw it. Also, freeze some of your pesto in ice cube trays. That way you can easily pop a flavorful nugget or two into soups, sauces, and stews. + One more thing: While pesto purists prefer using a mortar and pestle to create their perfections, I use the food processor for these recipes (a blender also works). I find it faster and easier, and I can make a larger quantity.

TRADITIONAL PESTO
Makes about 1 cup

2 TABLESPOONS PINE NUTS, RAW OR
LIGHTLY TOASTED IN A DRY SKILLET
2 MEDIUM GARLIC CLOVES, MINCED
(1^1/$_2$ FIRMLY PACKED TEASPOONS)
1^1/$_2$ TO 2 CUPS PACKED FRESH BASIL
LEAVES
^{1}/$_2$ CUP OR MORE EXTRA-VIRGIN OLIVE OIL
^{1}/$_2$ CUP FRESHLY GRATED PARMESAN OR
OTHER HARD ITALIAN CHEESE

In a food processor, pulse the pine nuts with the garlic, basil, and olive oil until combined. Add the cheese and pulse until smooth (or stir it in by hand before serving). Scrape the pesto into a bowl.

VARIATION:
For **LEMON BASIL PESTO,** follow the recipe for Traditional Pesto, adding 2 tablespoons of fresh lemon juice and 2 to 3 teaspoons of minced lemon zest with the garlic. Then proceed as directed.

RED BASIL AND SUN-DRIED TOMATO PESTO

Makes about 1 cup

2 TABLESPOONS PINE NUTS, RAW OR
   LIGHTLY TOASTED IN A DRY SKILLET
2 MEDIUM GARLIC CLOVES, MINCED
   (1¹/2 FIRMLY PACKED TEASPOONS)
1¹/2 CUPS PACKED FRESH OPAL BASIL
   LEAVES
3 TABLESPOONS MINCED SUN-DRIED
   TOMATOES
¹/2 CUP EXTRA-VIRGIN OLIVE OIL
¹/4 CUP PLUS 2 TABLESPOONS FRESHLY
   GRATED PARMESAN CHEESE
COARSE SALT, PREFERABLY KOSHER, AND
   FRESHLY GROUND PEPPER

In a food processor, pulse the pine nuts with the garlic, basil, tomatoes, and olive oil until combined. Add the cheese and pulse until smooth. Scrape the pesto into a bowl. Taste and adjust the seasoning with salt and pepper.

PISTACHIO PESTO

Makes about ²/3 cup

¹/2 CUP SHELLED, UNSALTED PISTACHIOS
2 MEDIUM GARLIC CLOVES, MINCED
   (1¹/2 FIRMLY PACKED TEASPOONS)
2 CUPS PACKED FRESH BASIL LEAVES
¹/4 CUP PLUS 2 TABLESPOONS EXTRA-
   VIRGIN OLIVE OIL
¹/4 CUP FRESHLY GRATED PARMESAN
   CHEESE
COARSE SALT, PREFERABLY KOSHER, AND
   FRESHLY GROUND PEPPER

In a food processor, pulse the pistachios with the garlic, basil, and olive oil until combined. Add the cheese and pulse until smooth. Scrape the pesto into a bowl. Taste and adjust the seasoning with salt and pepper.

BASIL MINT PESTO

Makes about $^2/_3$ cup

2 TABLESPOONS PINE NUTS, RAW OR
    LIGHTLY TOASTED IN A DRY SKILLET
2 MEDIUM GARLIC CLOVES, MINCED
    ($1^1/_2$ FIRMLY PACKED TEASPOONS)
1 CUP PACKED FRESH BASIL LEAVES
1 CUP PACKED FRESH MINT LEAVES
$^1/_4$ CUP PLUS 2 TABLESPOONS EXTRA-
    VIRGIN OLIVE OIL
$^1/_4$ CUP FRESHLY GRATED PARMESAN
    CHEESE
COARSE SALT, PREFERABLY KOSHER, AND
    FRESHLY GROUND PEPPER

In a food processor, pulse the pine nuts with the garlic, basil, mint, and olive oil until combined. Add the cheese and pulse until smooth. Scrape the pesto into a bowl. Taste and adjust the seasoning with salt and pepper.

WALNUT OREGANO PESTO

Makes about $^3/_4$ cup

$^1/_2$ CUP WALNUT HALVES
2 MEDIUM GARLIC CLOVES, MINCED
    ($1^1/_2$ FIRMLY PACKED TEASPOONS)
$^1/_2$ CUP PACKED FRESH OREGANO LEAVES
$^1/_4$ CUP EXTRA-VIRGIN OLIVE OIL
3 TABLESPOONS HEAVY (WHIPPING) CREAM
$^1/_4$ CUP FRESHLY GRATED PARMESAN
    CHEESE
COARSE SALT, PREFERABLY KOSHER, AND
    FRESHLY GROUND PEPPER

In a food processor, pulse the walnuts with the garlic, oregano, olive oil, and cream until combined. Add the cheese and pulse until smooth. Scrape the pesto into a bowl. Taste and adjust the seasoning with salt and pepper.

GARLIC BUTTERS TO SPREAD OR MELT

The next time you want to elevate simple grilled foods to party status or give family night vegetables some extra zest, top them with one of these compound garlic butters. Like a savvy restaurant chef, you'll have a finishing sauce in the time it takes to melt a pat of butter. Spread the joy! + To chill garlic butters for future use, roll each into a log (using plastic wrap to avoid a mess), wrap tightly, refrigerate, and enjoy within 2 days, or freeze for up to 3 weeks.

TARRAGON GARLIC BUTTER

Makes about $1/2$ cup
Bright and lively on vegetables, grilled chicken, fish, and even pasta.

$1/3$ TO $1/2$ CUP CHOPPED FRESH TARRAGON
    LEAVES

1 LARGE GARLIC CLOVE, MINCED (ABOUT
    $11/2$ FIRMLY PACKED TEASPOONS)

$11/2$ TEASPOONS MINCED SHALLOT

$1/2$ TO $3/4$ TEASPOON COARSE SALT,
    PREFERABLY KOSHER

2 TABLESPOONS EXTRA-VIRGIN OLIVE
    OIL

1 TABLESPOON WHITE WINE

$1/2$ CUP (1 STICK) UNSALTED BUTTER, AT
    ROOM TEMPERATURE

In a mini-prep processor, combine the tarragon, garlic, shallot, and salt until blended. Add the olive oil and process to a coarse paste. Add the wine and butter and blend thoroughly. Spoon the butter onto a piece of plastic wrap, and shape it into a small log. Wrap tightly, and refrigerate until firm. For longer storage, wrap a second time in foil. To use as a sauce, slice off a round, and let it melt on the hot food. To use as a spread, let the butter warm to room temperature.

ROSEMARY–ROASTED GARLIC BUTTER

Makes about $^{1}/_{2}$ cup

Delicious on anything at all (spoken like a true garlic lover).

1 MEDIUM HEAD GARLIC (2 TO
   2 $^{1}/_{2}$ OUNCES)
1 TO 2 TEASPOONS FINELY CHOPPED
   FRESH ROSEMARY
3 TABLESPOONS EXTRA-VIRGIN OLIVE
   OIL, DIVIDED
1 TEASPOON FRESH LEMON JUICE
$^{1}/_{2}$ CUP (1 STICK) UNSALTED BUTTER, AT
   ROOM TEMPERATURE
$^{1}/_{2}$ TEASPOON COARSE SALT, PREFERABLY
   KOSHER

Preheat the oven to 350°F.

Slice off the top of the head of garlic to expose the tips of the cloves. Place the head, root side down, in a small ovenproof dish. Sprinkle with the rosemary, then drizzle 1 tablespoon of the olive oil over the exposed tips. (If desired, a teaspoon of water also can be added, and so can a sprinkling of salt.) Cover tightly with foil. Bake until tender and golden, about 1 hour. Cool.

Squeeze the pulp from the garlic cloves and transfer with any residual oil to a mini-prep processor. Add the lemon juice, the remaining 2 tablespoons olive oil, butter, and salt, and process until blended. Spoon the butter onto a piece of plastic wrap, and shape into a small log. Wrap tightly, and refrigerate until firm. For longer storage, wrap a second time in foil. To use as sauce, slice off a round, and let it melt on the hot food. To use as spread, let the butter warm to room temperature.

SUMMER HERB GARLIC BUTTER

Makes about $1/2$ cup

Tasty on vegetables, hamburgers, and pasta.

1 LARGE GARLIC CLOVE, MINCED (ABOUT
    1$1/2$ FIRMLY PACKED TEASPOONS)

2 TABLESPOONS FINELY MINCED
    SHALLOT

$1/2$ TEASPOON GRATED LEMON ZEST

2 TABLESPOONS MINCED FRESH PARSLEY
    LEAVES

1 TABLESPOON MINCED FRESH THYME
    LEAVES

1 TABLESPOON MINCED FRESH
    MARJORAM LEAVES

1 TABLESPOON MINCED CHIVES

$1/4$ TEASPOON COARSE SALT, PREFERABLY
    KOSHER

$1/4$ TEASPOON LEMON PEPPER

2 TABLESPOONS EXTRA-VIRGIN OLIVE OIL

$1/2$ CUP (1 STICK) UNSALTED BUTTER, AT
    ROOM TEMPERATURE

In a mini-prep processor, combine the garlic, shallot, lemon zest, parsley, thyme, marjoram, chives, salt, and lemon pepper until blended. Add the olive oil and process to a coarse paste. Add the butter and blend thoroughly. Spoon the butter onto a piece of plastic wrap, and shape it into a small log. Wrap tightly, and refrigerate until firm. For longer storage, wrap a second time in foil. To use as a sauce, slice off a round, and let it melt on the hot food. To use as a spread, let the butter warm to room temperature.

NERVY, HEAVENLY GARLIC ICE CREAM

Makes about 1 pint

The ice-cold concoction before you looks like a rich and creamy vanilla bean ice cream. There's no hint of any extraordinary ingredient—that is, until you take your first bite. What happens next? You perceive a subtle scent of garlic, it lingers in your mouth, and then it's gone. So you take another bite . . . + I tasted my first garlic ice cream at the Gilroy Garlic Festival. The line for the ice cream booth was twice as long as any of the others. Curious, I waited in line, too. How could garlic and ice cream possibly add up to edible? + If you think about it, though, it's the combination of garlic and cream that makes so many savory sauces sublime. The same could be said for this daringly delicious dessert.

1 1/2 CUPS HALF-AND-HALF

1/4 TEASPOON FIRMLY PACKED MINCED
    GARLIC (1 PARTIAL CLOVE)

1/2 VANILLA BEAN, SPLIT LENGTHWISE

3 EGG YOLKS, AT ROOM TEMPERATURE

1/3 CUP SUGAR

In the top of a double boiler over simmering water, combine the half-and-half and garlic. Scrape the seeds from the vanilla bean into the half-and-half. Cook until small bubbles appear around the edges of the pan. Remove from the heat.

Meanwhile, in a medium bowl, whisk the egg yolks and sugar together until thick and smooth, 3 to 4 minutes. Slowly whisk 1/2 cup of the hot half-and-half into the yolk mixture, whisking constantly so that the eggs do not "cook" in the warm liquid. Then gradually whisk the yolk mixture into the hot half-and-half. Return the mixture to the double boiler and cook, stirring constantly, until the custard thickens, about 10 minutes. To check for doneness, dip a spoon into the mixture and draw your finger through the coat of custard on the back of the spoon. It should leave a trail. Remove from the heat and let cool to room temperature.

Strain the custard through a fine-mesh sieve, cover, and refrigerate for at least 2 hours or up to 3 days. Stir the mixture, then pour it into a small ice-cream maker. Freeze according to the manufacturer's instructions.

SOURCES

Essential books, Web sites, festivals, farms, and plant sources

These resources will help you in your quest for the best.

FESTIVALS

United States/East Coast

May

Garlic Fest
Fairfield, Connecticut
(203) 374-4503

August

Adams Garlic Festival
Pawcatuck, Connecticut
(860) 599-4241
adamsgarden@aol.com

Fox Run Vineyards Garlic Festival
Benton, New York
(800) 636-9786
www.foxrunvineyards.com

Keystone State Garlic & Herb Festival
Drums, Pennsylvania
(570) 788-3152
www.zanolininursery.com

August/Labor Day Weekend

Pocono Garlic Festival
Stroudsburg, Pennsylvania
(610) 381-3303
www.poconogarlic.com

Southern Vermont Garlic & Herb Festival
Wilmington, Vermont
(802) 368-7147
www.lovegarlic.com

September

Garlic Festival & Smoked Foods Extravaganza
Bar Harbor, Maine
(207) 288-2337
www.atlanticbrewing.com/events.html

North Quabbin Garlic & Arts Festival
Orange, Massachusetts
www.garlicandarts.org

Susquehanna Valley Garlic Festival
Milford, New York
(607) 432-8442
mrowley@stny.rr.com

Hudson Valley Garlic Festival
Saugerties, New York
(845) 246-3090
www.hvgf.org

October

Virginia Wine & Garlic Festival
Amherst, Virginia
(434) 946-5168
www.rebecwinery.com/vwgf.htm

November

Delray Beach Garlic Fest
Delray Beach, Florida
(561) 274-4663
www.dbgarlicfest.com

United States/Midwest

September

"Garlic Is Life" Symposium & Festival
Tulsa, Oklahoma
(918) 446-7522
www.garlicislife.com

United States/West Coast

June

Northwest Garlic Festival
Ocean Park, Washington
(888) 751-9354
www.opwa.com

July

Gilroy Garlic Festival
Gilroy, California
(408) 842-1625
www.gilroygarlicfestival.com

August

Elephant Garlic Festival
North Plains, Oregon
(888) 771-3708
www.funstinks.com

Arlington Garlic & Music Festival
Arlington, Washington
(360) 435-8577
www.garlicfestival.net

Okanogan River Garlic Festival
Tonasket, Washington
(509) 422-6940
www.filareefarm.com/fest.html

Canada

August

South Cariboo Garlic Festival
Forest Grove, British Columbia
(877) 397-2518
www.kariboofarms.com/garlic1.html

County Garlic Festival
Picton, Ontario
(613) 476-5943
www.countygarlicfestival.ca

Garlic Is Great Festival
Milton, Ontario
(888) 307-3276
www.garlicisgreat.ca

Canadian Garlic Festival
Sudbury, Ontario
(705) 673-7404
www.ukranianseniors.com

United Kingdom

August

Isle of Wight Garlic Festival
Isle of Wight
+44 (0) 1983 863566
www.garlicfestival.co.uk

FARMS AND GARLIC SOURCES
Many small farms either do not have the ability to mass-market or choose not to do so. Some have Web sites, others have mail-order catalogs, and many simply sell to their local markets (so be sure to check out the garlic at your local farmers' market).

Bobba-Mike's Garlic Farm
P.O. Box 261
Orrville, OH 44667
(330) 855-1141
www.garlicfarm.com
Catalog available online or by mail.

W.A. Burpee
Warminster, PA 18974
www.burpee.com
Catalog available online or by mail

Filaree Farm
182 Conconully Highway
Okanogan, WA 98840
www.filareefarm.com
Catalog available online or by mail. Web site includes garlic-growing tips.

Garlic Seed Foundation
Rose Valley Farm
Rose, NY 14542
www.garlicseedfoundation.info/
Catalog available online or by mail. Web site includes garlic classifications and resource listings.

Gourmet Garlic Gardens
Bangs, Texas
www.gourmetgarlicgardens.com
Bob Anderson is in the forefront of developing garlic that will grow in the South. Web site includes tips, recipes, gifts, and various articles.

Nichols Garden Nursery
1190 Old Salem Road NE
Albany, OR 97321
www.nicholsgardennursery.com
Catalog available online or by mail. Web site includes garlic tips and recipes.

Seed Savers Exchange
3076 N. Winn Road
Decorah, IA 52101
www.seedsaversexchange.com
Heirloom and organic garlic available online or by mail.

Yucca Ridge Farm
46050 Weld County Road 13
Fort Collins, CO 80524
(800) 854-7219
www.thegarlicstore.com
> Catalog available online or by mail. Web site includes garlic classifications, growing tips, recipes, resources, and more.

BOOKS

Aaron, Chester. *The Great Garlic Book.* Berkeley: Ten Speed Press, 1997.
> Includes numerous color photographs of various softneck and hardneck garlic varieties.

Griffith, Linda and Fred. *Garlic, Garlic, Garlic.* New York: Houghton Mifflin, 1998.
> Informative text, tips, and recipes.

Harris, Lloyd J. *The Book of Garlic.* Berkeley: Aris Books, revised 1979.
> Everything you ever wanted to know about garlic—and more! Detailed folklore, medical data, remedies, recipes, and trivia.

Harris, Lloyd J. *The Garlic Lover's Handbook.* Berkeley: Aris Books, 1986.
> More garlic wisdom, poetry, folklore, growing tips, history, and minutiae.

Ody, Penelope. *The Complete Medicinal Herbal.* London: Dorling Kindersley, 1993.
> An illustrated practical guide to the healing properties of herbs. Informative text on garlic and its medicinal applications.

GREAT GARLIC WEB SITES
> An Internet search engine will yield a multitude of garlic references. Here are a few terrific Web sites that provide useful information, goods, and services.

www.filareefarm.com
Filaree Farm
> Includes garlic growing tips, articles, books, and links.

www.mistral.co.uk/garlic
The Garlic Information Center
> An international information service reporting the medicinal benefits of garlic.

www.garlicislife.com
"Garlic Is Life" Symposium & Festival
> Includes garlic growing tips and recipes, history and lore, books, and links.

www.thegarlicstore.com
The Garlic Store.com
> A one-stop garlic Web site. All things garlic (including videos and DVDs) are available, along with garlic classifications, growing tips, recipes, resources, and more.

INDEX

TABLE OF EQUIVALENTS

The exact equivalents in the following tables have been rounded for convenience.

LIQUID/DRY MEASURES

U.S.	METRIC
1/4 TEASPOON	1.25 MILLILITERS
1/2 TEASPOON	2.5 MILLILITERS
1 TEASPOON	5 MILLILITERS
1 TABLESPOON (3 TEASPOONS)	15 MILLILITERS
1 FLUID OUNCE (2 TABLESPOONS)	30 MILLILITERS
1/4 CUP	60 MILLILITERS
1/3 CUP	80 MILLILITERS
1/2 CUP	120 MILLILITERS
1 CUP	240 MILLILITERS
1 PINT (2 CUPS)	480 MILLILITERS
1 QUART (4 CUPS, 32 OUNCES)	960 MILLILITERS
1 GALLON (4 QUARTS)	3.84 LITERS
1 OUNCE (BY WEIGHT)	28 GRAMS
1 POUND	454 GRAMS
2.2 POUNDS	1 KILOGRAM

LENGTH

U.S.	METRIC
1/8 INCH	3 MILLIMETERS
1/4 INCH	6 MILLIMETERS
1/2 INCH	12 MILLIMETERS
1 INCH	2.5 CENTIMETERS

OVEN TEMPERATURE

FAHRENHEIT	CELSIUS	GAS
250	120	1/2
275	140	1
300	150	2
325	160	3
350	180	4
375	190	5
400	200	6
425	220	7
450	230	8
475	240	9
500	260	10